KRIS KROHN

with STEPHEN PALMER

The

CONSCIOUS
CREATOR

6 LAWS FOR MANIFESTING
YOUR MASTERPIECE LIFE

SB PRESS

Published by Strongbrook Press
531 East 770 North
Orem, UT 84097
www.strongbrook.com

For ordering information or special discounts for bulk purchases, please contact Strongbrook Press at 531 East 770 North, Orem, UT 84097, www.strongbrook.com.

Design and composition by Greenleaf Book Group LLC
Cover design by Greenleaf Book Group LLC

Publisher's Cataloging-In-Publication Data
(Prepared by The Donohue Group, Inc.)
Krohn, Kris.
  The conscious creator : 6 laws for manifesting your masterpiece life / Kris Krohn, with Stephen Palmer.—1st ed.
    p. ; cm.
  Includes bibliographical references.
  ISBN: 978-0-9859677-0-3
  1. Self-realization. 2. Spiritual life. 3. Success. 4. Parables. I. Palmer, Stephen, 1976—II. Title.
BF637.S4 K76 2012   2012945322
158.1

Part of the Tree Neutral® program, which offsets the number of trees consumed in the production and printing of this book by taking proactive steps, such as planting trees in direct proportion to the number of trees used: www.treeneutral.com

Printed in the United States of America on acid-free paper

12 13 14 15 16 17   10 9 8 7 6 5 4 3 2 1

First Edition

TreeNeutral®

For my wife, Kalenn, who put her faith in me when these laws were still unproven in our life, and for my children, who (I hope) will be among the greatest beneficiaries.

AUTHOR'S NOTE

This book reads a lot like a work of fiction. But while the characters and the situations are not real, this isn't a novel. It's a parable, a story that teaches principles. And this parable will help you become who you were meant to become—it will help you live your True Purpose.

Millions of people are unhappy in their job or career, and would be much happier and of much more value to other people if they were doing something else. Some people know what their True Purpose is; others don't. But everyone can learn from the experience of Shaun Porter, the main character in this tale, as he applies the Six Laws of Conscious Creation and becomes a Conscious Creator.

ONE

Shaun realized he should have seen it coming. Amanda had seemed aloof and distracted for weeks. Still, nothing had prepared him for her devastating e-mail. Hadn't everything been going smoothly? Wasn't he a model of dependability, financial security, and faithfulness?

He wondered vaguely if he would have taken Amanda's parting words better in person.

His accounting firm had sent him to a three-day conference, and he'd endured two long, boring days of meetings. Though Shaun appreciated the job security, being a CPA was hardly a passion for him. He did it out of a sense duty and a belief that the "good life" is the product of sticking with a reliable job and company and saving religiously. That's how it was done by the people he looked up to, and he had it all planned out. But after four years of number crunching, he was beginning to wonder how long he'd last. On top of the daily grind of his job, there was this tiresome conference and now Amanda's devastating e-mail. The foundations of Shaun's world were shaken.

He sat alone and numb at his lunch table, staring blankly at the floor.

His fellow attendees were long gone, sitting in various breakout sessions. He lifted his cell phone and reread the e-mail for about the fifteenth time.

Dear Shaun,

I'm truly sorry for not doing this in person. The truth is that I still love you, and I was afraid I wouldn't be able to follow through with it. Please know that this hurts me as much as it hurts you.

I need to move on. I can't wait any longer for you to decide. I want to be with you. I want to have a family with you. But after two years of you avoiding even a conversation about this, I've come to the sad realization that it's never going to happen. You know my life's motto, and I worry that if I don't do this now, I will regret it. If you're not ready for marriage now, I doubt you will ever be.

When I first met you, I was drawn to your sense of responsibility. I felt like I could really depend on you—and that was true. But what really made me fall in love with you was the passion you revealed to me that night you told me about your trip to Europe. You were so energetic and alive. I saw a light in you I'd never seen before. Sadly, I've been waiting ever since for that passion to resurface.

I know you're afraid of what might happen in the future. So am I. Life is risky. Marriage is risky. But some risks are worth taking. You're worth the risk to me, but you obviously don't feel the same.

I appreciate your sense of duty, your thoughtfulness and planning. I just wish that sometimes you'd live a little more for passion and a little less for duty. I need you to be truly ALIVE, to go for what you really want, to accept whatever consequences may come and just keep moving forward. But as long as you're just following your plan to the letter and worrying about any slight deviation from that plan, you and I can't progress.

I wish you the best. I sincerely hope you'll find someone who fits your plan better than I do.

Amanda

As the shock wore off, anger set in. *Aren't I what every woman wants—a reliable guy with a secure job and a promising career?* he thought. *Haven't I been good to her? Can't she see what a good life I can give her—someday?* He felt betrayed by the very qualities he thought she should appreciate most in him. *And why is she in such a hurry? She's seen what spontaneity has done to my family. Doesn't she know that* passion *is just a nice-sounding word for* escaping responsibility, *that chasing dreams just leads to dead ends?*

Shaun stood abruptly, shoved his cell phone into his pocket, and strode into the hallway. He needed something to distract his mind, and suffering through more dry presentations by stuffy CPAs was the last thing he wanted to do. As he walked down the hall, not knowing where he was headed, he heard a boisterous crowd in an adjoining conference room. It was the same group he'd been hearing the whole time he'd been at the conference, and he wondered again who they were and what they were so excited about.

On a whim, he ducked in, took a seat in the back, and surveyed the room. An energetic, middle-aged man commanded the stage. His silver hair and warm smile gave him an almost grandfatherly appearance, but his angular features and dark, piercing eyes hinted that there was steel in him. His audience hung on every word and cheered frequently. The atmosphere was electric.

But when Shaun's eye fell on the sign at the entrance, which he had missed in his distraught stupor, he groaned inwardly. *Great, a network marketing party. Just what I need right now: another reminder that Amanda wants me to be more like my footloose and fancy-free father.* He started to leave, but something the speaker was saying held his attention.

"Our ancestors handed us a feast of economic possibilities on silver platters. They laid the foundations. Their blood, sweat, tears, and sacrifices have become our privileges, opportunities, and blessings. All we have to do is show up and partake of that feast."

Ah well, thought Shaun, *it's not like I have anything better to do.* He settled in to his seat and listened to what seemed to be a stirring speech.

"But most of us choke down the stale bread of compromise, mediocrity, and security," the man continued, "because we're afraid. We're afraid of sticking our necks out. We're afraid people will make fun of us. We're afraid of failure. We're afraid we don't have what it takes. We somehow think that dutiful work for corporations is safer than following our bliss and living our dreams.

"You think succeeding in business *today* is hard? Try suffering through Valley Forge. Try swimming through bodies and blood on D-Day. Try hacking out a farm in virgin wilderness, with no government subsidies, with nothing but your muscles, your tools, your livestock, and the vision of a better life beating in your heart. The freedom we were handed is worthless if we don't exercise it. Those who went before us gave us the opportunity to be free, but if we don't take that opportunity, we're not much more than well-fed, comfortable slaves. Their sacrifices were in vain if we cower in our corporate cubicles, waiting for others to lead, to build, to innovate, to dream."

The crowd raved as the speaker paused for a breath and a drink of water. Shaun, too, was mesmerized, and for the moment he forgot all about his heartache.

The speaker continued, slower and calmer now. "Today you've been given the Six Laws of Conscious Creation to help you live up to your heritage, achieve your dreams, and become truly free. But you must live those laws with faith, courage, and persistence. They aren't a magic wand you can just wave over your life and suddenly, with no effort, everything becomes just the way you've dreamed it. Living your passion and achieving your dreams is not an easy path. It's a path full of struggle. It comes with its share of heartache. But it's what you were born for. It's the only path worthy of your heritage. And with all my heart and soul, I promise you this: The journey is worth it."

With that, the speaker left the stage, and the crowd erupted. Shaun remained seated, the only one in the room who was not standing. He was stunned by what he'd just heard. He felt personally accused by the speaker's words, and that was exactly how Amanda's e-mail had made him feel too.

And then it dawned on him why it hurt: It was true, every bit of it. Amanda's e-mail and what he'd just heard from this charismatic speaker—they both hit the bull's-eye. He had always considered his views about how to live *wise*. Now he knew he had just been living *scared*.

TWO

As Shaun drove home that night, the shock and anger he'd been feeling turned to grief. He prepared for bed, staring long and hard in the mirror, deep in thought. Ordinarily, his blond hair, blue eyes, and quick smile made him look younger than he was, but tonight he looked older, worn out from his distress.

The next day, he dutifully returned to work, and grief settled in to depression. Days crawled by, a grim sludge of pointless numbers and oppressive forms. The long-term vision that had upheld him in his methodical work had deserted him along with Amanda, and now he was seriously questioning not only his career choices but also his core ideas on how to live life. He felt uprooted. Without the clarity and assurance he had always felt, what was he left with?

A week later, as Shaun listlessly pecked at dinner while staring at the TV, a light pierced his clouded mind. *What were those six laws the speaker mentioned? And could they help me get out of this funk?* But still too drained to act, Shaun let the thought pass without taking it too seriously, and the light dimmed. *Besides,* he thought, *what could a network marketing guru teach me? To end up like my father? No thanks.*

Two more weeks dragged by. The thought of the six laws periodically pestered Shaun's thoughts, an internal voice trying desperately to burn through his self-absorbed fog. Finally, he responded to the voice by sitting down at his computer to do a Google search. The term *six laws of conscious creation* brought up nothing on the laws specifically, and he didn't know where else to begin his research. He couldn't even remember the guy's name. What was the company name he'd seen on the sign in the conference room? He wracked his brain, tried a few searches, and came up empty. At last he found something that looked familiar: a marketing company selling health and wellness products. He navigated to the FOUNDER page and saw a picture of the speaker he'd seen at the conference: Stewart Baker. *One step closer,* he thought.

But how could he contact this Stewart Baker? He must be insulated by layers of handlers. It would be futile to try the company's CONTACT page. Shaun Googled *Stewart Baker,* which predictably generated tons of results, but not what he was looking for. He jumped back to the company website and sifted through a few pages, almost ready to give up, until he landed on the EVENTS page and saw it: Stewart Baker was scheduled to speak at an event in Phoenix on an upcoming Saturday, one month from now. The venue was just a half hour's drive from Shaun's house.

Coincidence? Luck? *Nah, just plain chance,* thought Shaun. He wondered if they'd even let him through the door or if he'd have to join the company just to get a shot at talking to Stewart. He scheduled the event in his phone and continued searching. Thirty minutes later, the event was still his only lead on what these six laws were all about. He would have to do it.

Shaun decided on a plan: to endure the event, then see if he could approach Stewart afterward. He smirked and thought: *If only Dad could see me now. He'd be so proud of me, going to a rah-rah, follow-your-dreams, be-all-you-can-be manipulation fest.*

Feeling relieved that he had at least made a start, Shaun spent the next month burying himself in work. In the evenings he exercised, and on weekends he went mountain biking or hiking to resist the undertow of self-pitying thoughts—and to stop thinking about Amanda's laugh.

Above all he cooked. Although it wasn't nearly as much fun without someone to share the meals with, he became increasingly engrossed in doing what he loved most. He never would have called cooking a "passion"; to him, it was more of a hobby. But cooking brought him the peace and joy he never really felt while doing anything else. He was mostly unconscious of those feelings, though, because they were just so natural. He felt at home in the kitchen, and when he was cooking, he lost all track of time.

The evening of the Stewart Baker event arrived. Shaun dressed business casual and arrived fifteen minutes early. He maneuvered his way past the greeters at the door, taking advantage of a moment when they were distracted. He took a seat in the back and braced himself for the cheerleading session to begin. He impatiently hung on through the first hour of awards and minor speakers, amusing himself by counting how many times the crowd applauded.

Finally, Stewart was up. Once again Shaun found himself opening up to this man's persona and soaking up every word. Stewart seemed to him a rare mix of zeal and authenticity, charisma and substance. Strangely, the man didn't seem as though he were born to be on stage, yet he captivated his audience with depth and honesty that disarmed Shaun.

Stewart shared a classic rags-to-riches story of being raised on the wrong side of the tracks in Oklahoma City, a single child of a single mother.

He spoke of going hungry, fending for himself, wearing holey shoes and patched jeans, being mocked at school. Stewart's eyes glowed as he spoke of his mother, a fiercely independent woman who pounded integrity into him. He said he grew up with a chip on his shoulder, which led to frequent fights in school.

At age sixteen, Stewart started working for a local organic farmer, Wayne Christofferson. Wayne was a gentle soul, full of love and wisdom. He took Stewart under his wing and mentored him through his high school years. Stewart developed a love and respect for nature, and he got interested in growing food. Learning the rhythms of nature helped calm his anger, and he stopped fighting at school. When Stewart graduated, an anonymous donor paid his way through college. Stewart had always known it was Wayne, and he had never forgotten that profound act of service.

At age twenty-two, Stewart had graduated with a business degree. He worked at a few companies for a couple of years before realizing he just wasn't cut out for corporate life. At age twenty-seven, he scraped together $5,000 to start his first company, which crashed and burned, as did his next three entrepreneurial attempts. But his next two businesses, including a natural foods company, were wildly successful, propelling him to cofound his direct sales company to share his passion for natural health with others.

Shaun was disappointed that Stewart did not list the six laws, but he thoroughly enjoyed Stewart's presentation. He admired Stewart's perseverance and the down-to-earth manner that reflected his legitimacy. Here was a man who had come through some fires. Shaun realized this wasn't smoke and mirrors; Stewart really knew how to succeed.

Stewart closed his speech. Once again, his sincerity and earnestness had captured the hearts of his audience. He stepped off the stage, and Shaun craned his neck to see through the crowd. Where was Stewart going? When he left through a side door, Shaun's heart sank. *I've waited a month to see him, and now I'm losing my chance,* he thought. He rushed out into the hall—and was relieved to see Stewart there.

"Mr. Baker!" Shaun called, breaking into a jog to catch him. Stewart turned and smiled as Shaun approached. "Mr. Baker," Shaun said again, and then he launched into his prepared speech. "You don't know me from Adam, and I'm not even in your company. But I heard you speak at a conference several weeks ago. I was at another conference in the same event center, but I stepped into yours on a whim and caught the last five minutes of your speech. You spoke of six laws, and ever since, I've been dying to know what those laws are. I tracked you down through your company website and saw that you were speaking in Phoenix tonight."

Shaun paused for breath and then continued, "I need to know what those six laws are. I just have this feeling that they're what I need in my life right now." Shaun's initial idea had been simply to ask Stewart to tell him his six laws right then and there, but now he found that the words gushed from his mouth almost involuntarily: "I know this is crazy, since you don't even know me, and I'm sure you get requests like this all the time, but . . . will you teach me your laws of creation?"

Stewart smiled graciously and extended his hand. "And you are?"

"I'm sorry. My name is Shaun Porter."

"Shaun, I can teach the six laws to anyone. But the real question is whether or not you'll pay the price to live them. Knowledge *in your head* is cheap. The real value comes from living truth *in your heart and actions.*"

"Yes, sir, I understand. But I think I'm ready. I've just . . . been trying to figure out a lot of things lately. I had my whole life planned out, but things have changed. I need some help to see more clearly and find the right path."

Stewart listened patiently, then said, "Shaun, I have one question that will tell me whether or not you're ready: Who are you, and what do you want to accomplish and become in your life?"

Shaun stammered, "I . . . I don't know. I mean, I thought I knew. I thought my plan was solid. Now you've got me thinking that it would be a huge mistake. But can't you help me figure that out?"

"Sorry, Shaun. No, I can't help you. No one can help you if you don't know who you are and where you want to go. If you don't know your destination, I might as well just point in any direction, because it doesn't really matter, does it?"

"Well, can't you at least tell me the six laws, and I can figure it out from there?" Shaun pleaded.

"No. I'm sorry. You're not ready for them. It would be a waste of my time and yours. But I truly wish you the best." Stewart shook Shaun's hand again and turned to leave.

Shaun stood there, deflated. He'd been waiting so long for this moment, and the rejection compounded his sorrows. "Mr. Baker," he called out in desperation, "isn't there *something* you can tell me to at least get me started in the right direction?"

Stewart stopped and turned. "Well, there is one clue I can give you. But after that, you're on your own. You're the only one who can know who you are and what you want." He pulled a card from his breast pocket and handed it to Shaun. "Good luck, Shaun."

Shaun looked at the card, which was stark white but for one strange word in black letters: *Satcitananda.*

"What the hell?" he muttered under his breath. When he looked up, Stewart was gone.

As Shaun walked to the parking garage, his frustration mounted. By the time he was on the road, he was downright angry. *What is it with that guy? Is he just not willing to talk to me because I'm not in his precious company, making him richer? The last thing I need is more mystical mumbo jumbo from selfish charlatans. These guys know just how to string you along, taking your money bit by bit until you're left with nothing but hollow platitudes that you repeat desperately to your family and friends, as if saying them enough times will actually make them true. Just ask my father.*

Disgusted, he grabbed the card from his pocket and flicked it out the window. He drove on, trying to convince himself that the card was nothing but a silly rabbit hole that would ultimately just lead to making more money for Stewart Baker. He didn't remember what it said, and he didn't care. But he couldn't ignore the soft but urgent voice inside: *What do you have to lose?*

It was true. What did he have to lose? What if the clue actually led to something important?

Shaun slammed on his brakes. The car behind him swerved, horn bellowing, narrowly avoiding a collision. Shaun flipped a U-turn and drove back to the spot where he thought he had chucked the card. He pulled off the road and parked, then got out and began searching desperately on the road and in the weeds along the shoulder.

After fifteen minutes he returned to his car, feeling defeated and mentally kicking himself for his stupidity. His one clue was gone.

THREE

Monday morning lumbered into Shaun's gloomy consciousness. He lugged his body out of bed, performed his morning routine robotically, and headed off to work. He sagged into his cubicle, late for the first time in four years. He stared at the imposing stack of papers on his desk, lost in thought.

This is what I have to look forward to for the next thirty-six years? he brooded. *How did Uncle Frank do it? Did he ever have days like this?*

Frank was the exact opposite of his brother, Robert—Shaun's father—and Shaun had admired him since his teenage years. In fact, he had chosen accounting because of Frank's example. Frank was studious, meticulous, methodical, patient, and wise. A hard worker and diligent saver, he retired after working for the same accounting firm for forty years, and now he spent his days golfing, traveling, and volunteering in his community. His had been a stable and safe life throughout, and Shaun had tried to emulate that.

Shaun pulled the top folder from the pile and willed himself to open it and subject himself to the work, dutiful as always. *Back to the grind . . .*

Thus passed two weeks, Shaun's only reprieve being his evening experiments in the kitchen. Every day he was tempted to call or e-mail Amanda, but his pride kept him from doing that.

One Wednesday morning, Michele, a fellow accountant, approached his cubicle. "Hey, Shaun, you got a minute?"

Shaun glanced up from his stack of folders. "Sure, what's up?"

Michele seemed nervous. "So I'm kind of new at this, but I wanted to tell you about an opportunity. I've been taking this health supplement for the past three months, and I've had a lot more energy, I've been sleeping better, and I've even found that I remember things better."

Oh, great, thought Shaun, *here comes the oh-so-predictable pitch.*

Seeing Shaun's face change from curious to smug, Michele rushed her prepared speech. "But what I've been even more excited about is the opportunity to sell the product and earn extra income. In fact, I'm hoping to completely replace my job income within six months."

"I'm sorry," Shaun said, "but I'm going to stop you right there. I've heard it all before. I respect what you're doing, but it's just not my thing."

"Okay," Michele said, trying to remain cheerful. "Here, can I just leave you with a card in case you change your mind?"

"Sure," Shaun said. He tossed the card onto his desk without looking at it.

Michele left, and as Shaun turned back to his work, he glanced at the card. Written on it, he was astonished to discover, was the name of Stewart Baker's company.

Shaun grabbed the card, scrambled out of his cubicle, and scurried down the hall. "Michele, wait!" She paused and turned. "Hey, is Stewart Baker one of the founders of your company?" he asked.

"Yeah! How do you know him?" Michele asked.

"Well, it's a long story," Shaun replied. "Let's just say . . . I think he has my keys. Listen, I know this is a long shot, but I don't suppose you have any contact information for him, do you?"

"Actually, I do," Michele said. "I'm in his downline, and I have his e-mail address. In fact, he just responded to an e-mail from me last week. I've even been to his house." Misreading Shaun's interest, she continued, "He's been so helpful and generous as I've been starting out. That's something I really appreciate about the company. You really should check it out."

"Maybe I will sometime," Shaun deflected. "Can I start by getting Stewart's e-mail address?"

Michele wrote it down, and Shaun rushed back to his desk to compose a message.

Mr. Baker,

You might not remember me. I caught up with you after an event in Phoenix a couple of weeks ago and asked you to mentor me on your six laws of creation. You said you couldn't help me, but you left me with a card that had some weird word on it.

    Unfortunately, I've lost the card and I can't remember the word. Would you please e-mail me the word? I'd like to figure out what it means.

Sincerely,
Shaun Porter

Shaun was surprised to find a response in his in-box the next day.

Shaun,

Of course I remember you—the desperate young man in search of a new path in life. I'm guessing by the fact that you lost my card that you don't actually want a new life that badly. I'm sorry, but I can't waste clues on dabblers. My time and effort are reserved for those truly committed to a masterpiece life.

Regrettably,
Stewart

Shaun wanted to be angry, but he knew he couldn't blame Stewart—especially since he hadn't been exactly truthful in his e-mail. Crestfallen, he tried to get back to work. But now he was plagued even more by the mysterious word.

Inspired by an idea, Shaun went to Michele's office. "Hey, Michele, have you ever heard of Stewart Baker's Six Laws of Conscious Creation?" he asked.

"I've heard people in the company talk a little about them, but I haven't learned them yet," she responded.

"I heard about them when I walked into the last five minutes of a speech he gave a few weeks ago," Shaun explained. "Then, two weeks ago, I went to one of the company events and spoke with Stewart after the meeting. He wouldn't share his laws with me, but he handed me a card that had a weird word on it. It looked like it was in another language. He said it was some clue. Would you know anything about that? Have you ever heard anyone in the company talk about anything like that?"

Michele shook her head. "No, it doesn't ring a bell. Don't you still have the card?"

"Uh, no," Shaun admitted. "I actually asked Stewart to mentor me, and he turned me down. I got mad, so I threw the card out the window on my drive home that night. I know, it was stupid."

"I wish I could help you," said Michele, "but I don't know anything about it."

Shaun had struck out. He would have to find guidance elsewhere.

After work that day he drove to a bookstore and browsed the self-help and business sections, choosing a handful of books that looked interesting. He started reading that evening, and it became a habit—he would read every evening for an hour before going to bed. Because of past experiences, Shaun resisted much of what he read. But some of it started making sense.

The recurring idea that stood out to him most was living life on purpose. Previously, had anyone asked, he would have said yes, he absolutely lived on purpose. After all, he had a plan and was steadfastly carrying it out. But as Shaun was slowly realizing, his plan was basically a script written not by him but by others. He had been doing what he thought he *should* be doing instead of something that he really *wanted* to do. He had been wanting what he thought he should be wanting—instead of wanting what he really needed.

Shaun knew he needed more clarity. Just as Stewart Baker had said, he needed to know who he was and what he truly wanted. As the days went by, he began to be much more introspective than he'd ever been, taking long walks and journaling. A few weeks passed, and although he was continually discontented with his job, he was enjoying learning more about himself.

He arrived home from work one evening, flipped on the TV, and went into the kitchen to cook dinner. As usual, he lost track of time and wasn't paying attention to what was happening on TV. But suddenly, a strange word from the TV program pierced his consciousness. He dropped his knife, grabbed the remote, and turned the volume up. A bearded and robed man was saying something about enlightenment.

"As I said earlier, this essence of Universal Consciousness is expressed in three Sanskrit words: *sat, cit, ananda*. As you achieve *satcitananda,* you transcend duality and become your highest spiritual self."

"That's it!" Shaun exclaimed. "That was the word on Stewart's card!"

But the program had come to an end, and Shaun was left hanging. Frantically, he jumped online and Googled several spelling variations. Finally, he got a hit, on Wikipedia:

> *Saccidānanda, Satchidananda,* or *Sat-cit-ānanda* [pronounced suht-chit-ah-nuhn-duh] is a compound of three Sanskrit words, *sat, cit,* and *ānanda,* meaning *existence (truth, the eternal), consciousness,* and *bliss,* respectively. The expression comes from Hinduism and is used in yoga and other schools of Indian philosophy to describe the nature of Brahman as experienced by a fully liberated yogi or saint . . . Yoga describes the essence of Universal Consciousness as *Satcitananda,* which means existence, consciousness, and absolute bliss.

Shaun was befuddled. He had no interest in becoming an enlightened yogi or a saint; he just wanted to live a happy, fulfilling life and to make a difference. And Stewart Baker hadn't struck him as particularly mystical, but rather much more grounded. Still, there was no doubt that this was the word he'd seen on Stewart's card.

Shaun wrote the word *satcitananda* on a 3 x 5 card, along with the three-word interpretation: *truth, consciousness, bliss.* Yet despite stumbling upon Stewart's clue once again, Shaun felt more lost than ever.

FOUR

Shaun pondered those three words—*truth, consciousness, bliss*—for days. He researched everything he could find on the Sanskrit term *satcitananda*. He couldn't imagine that Stewart was trying to lead a bunch of network marketers to spiritual enlightenment after the Buddhist tradition. Or was he? Was Stewart Baker trying to build himself up as a guru? Or was there something more practical to this than Shaun realized?

Slowly, ideas began to form and dots began to connect. A tentative explanation revealed itself. It felt incomplete and ethereal, but it was starting to make enough sense that Shaun continued stumbling down the trail. He was anxious to get the full explanation from Stewart. He longed to be mentored by a man who seemed to have all the answers, while he himself was struggling just to make it through work every day.

In a flash of inspiration, Shaun knew what he was going to do. His practical side, which had ruled him for years, screamed that he was crazy. *Maybe so,* he thought. But as he'd heard before, straight from his internal voice, what did he have to lose?

The next day at the office, a Friday, he found Michele. "Michele, didn't you tell me you'd been to Stewart Baker's house?"

"Yes," she said, "he had a meeting there not too long ago with a group of associates. He actually has people over quite a bit."

"Where does he live?" Shaun asked.

"In California, about thirty minutes east of Fresno," she said. "Why do you ask?"

"Call me crazy, but I want to go see him personally. I've figured some things out, but I desperately need his insight and clarification. He'll probably just turn me away, but I've got to try something. Do you think he'd mind if you gave me his address?"

"Well," Michele hesitated, "I suppose it's okay. Like I said, he's always inviting people over, so he'd probably be okay with it."

Shaun scribbled the address down, left work early without giving an explanation, and went home. After packing enough for a couple of days, he gassed up his Camry and took off for Fresno. As he drove, the words *truth, consciousness, bliss* looped through his mind like a broken record. He made it as far as Bakersfield, where he stopped for the night. He got back on the road the next morning and pulled up to Stewart Baker's driveway at about eleven a.m.

As he turned onto the long, winding, tree-lined drive, Shaun was struck by a realization that he'd never even considered: Stewart might not be home. Anxious and steeled for the worst, he pulled up to the house, a Spanish-style mansion with whitewashed walls, an orange tile roof, gorgeous picture windows, and a grand entrance. The house stood on immaculate grounds with a commanding view of the forest valley below. It was like something Shaun had seen only in magazines and on TV. *Uncle Frank may have had security,* mused Shaun, *but he never lived like this.*

Nervousness gripped him again as he rang Stewart's doorbell. Half expecting a stiff-backed butler, Shaun was taken aback when Stewart himself answered the door.

"Well, if it isn't my lost and desperate friend, Shaun," Stewart exclaimed. "How in the world did you ever find me?"

"Please forgive me for barging in on you like this," Shaun gushed. "One of my coworkers is in your company. She's been to your house, and she told me where you live. I found the word you gave me, and it's been driving me nuts. I haven't been able to sleep much at all—I've been trying to figure it out. I still don't know if I understand why you use it as a clue, but I have some ideas. And I totally understand if you don't want to waste your time on me, but will you please just listen to my ideas and tell me if I'm on the right track or not?"

Stewart laughed and said, "I've got to give you credit. Come on in."

Shaun felt a rush of relief. "I can't thank you enough," he said.

Stewart escorted him down the hall and into an open room lined with bookshelves and with a big window that offered a spectacular view of the valley.

"Have a seat," Stewart said. "Would you like something to drink?"

"Yes, please," Shaun answered.

"Lemonade?"

"Sure."

Stewart left, then returned with a glass of lemonade, which he handed to Shaun. "You came all the way from Phoenix?"

Shaun grinned. "I did. I actually left work just as soon as I got your address. I've never done anything so crazy and spontaneous in my life, but I was afraid I'd chicken out if I didn't just do it. A friend of mine told me I should take more risks in life . . . so here I am."

"Shaun," Stewart said, "you'd be amazed at how little effort most people are willing to put forth to learn and grow, to achieve their ideal life. Driving out here took guts, and I admire you for it. So tell me, what have you figured out about *satcitananda*?"

Shaun began haltingly, "Like I said, I have no idea if I'm on the right track or not. And I really don't even have much to say, so you'll probably think my trip was silly."

Stewart dismissed his self-deprecating manner with a hand gesture.

Shaun continued, "So, I know it's a Sanskrit word made up of the three words 'truth,' 'consciousness,' and 'bliss.'"

Stewart nodded and waited patiently.

"I've been pondering the relationship between those three concepts for days," Shaun said. "As I understand it, truth is what *is*. Not what we think it is, not what we want it to be, but what just is. It is existence that transcends human perception—in other words, objective reality.

"Consciousness is how well we understand and relate with truth. The lower our consciousness, the more we don't understand truth. That frustrates us. Things don't work out for us like we want them to, and we can't accept that. Low consciousness leads to anger and bitterness and every other negative emotion. It makes us seek happiness in ways that can never bring happiness. And it leaves us with things that can actually make us addicted and destroy us."

The words began flowing easier and faster as Shaun warmed up to the topic and sensed Stewart's encouragement.

"And speaking of happiness, that's the end result of raising our consciousness. The more we raise our consciousness and align our actions with truth, the happier we become. So the path to bliss is to learn truth and live it as completely as we can, which raises our consciousness.

"But the problem is this: How can I really know what truth is? And how can I know that my consciousness is correct, that I'm really perceiving things accurately? I mean, I've had plenty of experiences where I thought for sure I was right, but as I got older and wiser, I realized how mistaken I was. In fact, that's why I'm here: I thought my life's plan was perfect, but now I know that life is not what I want. But I really don't know what I should do differently, so I'm just confused." Shaun finished speaking and looked to Stewart for answers.

"I'm impressed," Stewart said. "You've done a good job of thinking it through. And the problem you describe is quite common. But the answers to your questions lie within the relationship between the three concepts. Ever heard of Joseph Campbell?"

"I vaguely remember hearing the name in college," Shaun said.

"He was a scholar and teacher who spent his life studying myths and stories across all cultures," Stewart said. "He became popular for his studies on the hero's journey, a universal story that occurs in every culture in the world. I came across that word, '*satcitananda,*' in one of his books. It's interesting that you came to the same point as he did."

Stewart stood and went over to a bookshelf, returning with a book. He opened it to a marked passage and began reading:

Now, I came to this idea of bliss because in Sanskrit, which is the great spiritual language of the world, there are three terms that represent the brink, the jumping-off place to the ocean of transcendence: sat-chit-ananda. The word 'sat' means being. 'Chit' means consciousness. 'Ananda' means bliss or rapture. I thought, 'I don't know whether my consciousness is proper consciousness or not; I don't know whether what I know of my being is my proper being or not; but I do know where my rapture is. So let me hang on to rapture, and that will bring me both my consciousness and my being.

Stewart turned a few pages and continued quoting Campbell:

I even have a superstition that has grown on me as the result of invisible hands coming all the time—namely, that if you do follow your bliss, you put yourself on a kind of track that has been there all the while, waiting for you, and the life that you ought to be living is the one you are living. When you can see that, you begin to meet people who are in the field of your bliss, and they open the doors to you. I say, follow your bliss and don't be afraid, and doors will open where you didn't know they were going to be.

When Stewart put the book down, he said, "And that's the real clue to learning and living the Six Laws of Conscious Creation: *Follow your bliss.* I give people like you the word *'satcitananda'* just to test you, to see how badly you want to learn. Most people shrug it off as irrelevant mysticism, and hardly anyone ever comes back to me with anything intelligent from studying the word. But you've done a great job."

Shaun was ecstatic—he felt all the dots connecting. "Of course!" he exclaimed. "It all makes sense now. Following your bliss is the key to unlocking truth and higher consciousness." He pondered a moment, then frowned. "But what if you don't know what your bliss is? You said you couldn't help me if I didn't know who I was and what I wanted. So even though I understand this concept, I'm still not sure where I should go from here."

Stewart nodded. "I know what you mean. More often than not, following our bliss isn't that easy, because we're not consciously aware of it.

Most people are blind to their bliss because it comes from doing things that feel so natural to them that they don't even recognize their value. Sometimes it takes some outside perspective to help us recognize those things."

Shaun was hesitant to ask again. But he'd come this far, so what could it hurt? He started, "Mr. Baker—"

"Please," Stewart interrupted, "call me Stewart."

Shaun nodded. "Stewart," he pleaded, "what would it take to get you to mentor me, to teach me your six laws and help me really live them? I know that with your help, I can find my bliss and live the life I know I'm capable of. I'll pay you whatever you ask, even if it means dipping into my savings. And I promise to do whatever you tell me to do."

Stewart stared at him thoughtfully. "I'll tell you what: Your boldness in coming here earned you some points. Save your money. I'll teach you the first two laws on a trial basis. If I feel that you're listening and progressing, we can continue. Otherwise, I'm a busy man and there are plenty of other people to help."

Shaun was ecstatic. "Thank you so much! I promise I won't let you down."

"Well, if you don't live the laws, you won't be letting *me* down," Stewart said. "You'll be letting yourself down.

"Listen to me carefully now, Shaun," he continued, his voice low and earnest. "Do *not* underestimate these laws. If you actually live the laws, you'll receive power that you won't even comprehend. Winston Churchill said, 'Men occasionally stumble over the truth, but most of them pick themselves up and hurry off as if nothing ever happened.' If I share these laws with you, you won't be stumbling over truth. You'll be drinking it from a fire hose.

"These laws are infinitely bigger than your personal struggles, infinitely more powerful than just getting you out of a job you don't like. Underlying these laws is the power by which empires have been built. These laws are the source of mankind's greatest achievements, from cathedrals to skyscrapers . . . from exotic automobiles to jets . . . from landing on the moon to curing diseases . . . from cell phones to the Internet. These laws explain the greatest, most breathtaking masterpieces in art and music. They create monumental breakthroughs in science and technology. The most enlightened businesses are built on these laws. The most inspiring books were written by people who applied these laws.

"Shaun, these laws unleash the supreme power of manifestation. Do you get how deep this goes?"

"Well, I guess I have a general feel for it," Shaun said.

Stewart continued, "Shaun, I'm quite literally talking about the ability to manifest as a reality anything you desire. These laws allow a Conscious Creator to master the discipline of manifestation. *Manifesting* is turning your thoughts that are in alignment with your passion and purpose into physical reality. Conscious Creators are individuals who have developed the ability to manifest with faith, in their appropriate time and space, their desires that are in alignment with their True Purpose.

"A Conscious Creator knows he or she can dream, build, and achieve anything he or she wants—within natural laws, of course. Conscious Creators transcend limitations and overcome obstacles. They are relentlessly creative, innovative, and productive. Using the power of choice, they avoid being at the mercy of the winds of fortune and whims of luck. They are fueled by passion and driven by a clear purpose and a compelling vision. They know exactly who they are and what they want, and they're willing to pay the price to get it. But what the Conscious Creator wants isn't just about that individual; he or she strives to build something bigger than the self and to leave a lasting legacy.

"This is in contrast to the majority of people, who, as Oliver Wendell Holmes put it, 'die with their music still in them.' People who let life just happen to them, rather than choosing and consciously creating how they want their life to be. People who live by default rather than by design. People who think they're victims of circumstance, rather than heed the truth that they can choose their responses to *any* circumstances.

"This isn't to say that Conscious Creators are intrinsically worth more and merit better treatment than others. But they do enjoy their lives more. They serve more people and make a greater difference.

"The purpose of the six laws is to help you become a Conscious Creator. They help you overcome your doubts, fears, and limitations. When you become free of any thought that limits you, you are unlimited in your ability to create. And since each one of us was born to create, this leads to the highest levels of peace, joy, and fulfillment. More than just creating businesses, products, and services, Conscious Creators create and live their ideal life. Is this what you want?"

"Absolutely," Shaun quickly responded.

"And are you willing to pay the price?" Stewart asked.

"Yes," Shaun said, "but to be honest, I'm not entirely sure what that price is."

"Try living the laws and you'll find out soon enough," Stewart said. "And you'll also discover that talk is cheap. Nothing but experience will determine whether you're really willing to pay the price.

"Once you learn these laws, you can continue your dissatisfied life as if nothing had ever happened. Or you can apply the six laws to achieve a life you can't even dream of right now. The choice is yours. But I want you to understand the deep and inescapable responsibility of truth. Don't take this lightly. By learning these laws, you will have accepted a stewardship to live them and to be a light to others. The more light and truth you have, the greater your culpability if you don't live according to it. Do you understand this?"

"I think so," Shaun said soberly. "When do we start?"

"Well," Stewart said, "how about tomorrow? I've got some things to finish up today. Do you have a place to stay tonight, or were you planning on driving back to Phoenix?"

"To tell you the truth," Shaun said, "I hadn't really thought it through. I didn't imagine that I'd even make it this far, that I'd actually be sitting here with you."

"Well, then, it's solved," Stewart said. "You'll just have to stay with us. Go grab your bags and I'll show you to the guest room."

"Oh, I shouldn't, really," Shaun protested. "Not after just dropping in on you like this."

"Nonsense," Stewart said. "You think this house is just for my enjoyment? Get your bags."

Shaun gratefully did as he was told. Stewart got him settled in his room, then introduced him to his wife, Melanie, a youthful-looking, petite, and pretty brunette who exuded warmth and class. He then gave Shaun a tour of the property, inviting him to take advantage of the pool, exercise room, and theater. Shaun spent a restful afternoon lounging by the pool, browsing in the Bakers' library, and exploring wooded paths on the property. He joined the Bakers for a hearty dinner, and then he went to his room for the night.

Shaun thought he'd be too excited to sleep, but his long and furious drive had caught up to him and he drifted off blissfully.

FIVE

Morning peeked through Shaun's window. He stretched, smiling and contented. He couldn't remember the last time he'd slept so well. He was feeling peaceful; everything was going to work out perfectly, just as it should. He showered and dressed, and then ventured into the kitchen, where he found Stewart and Melanie getting ready to make breakfast.

"Good morning, Shaun," Melanie said. "Any special requests for breakfast? We were going to have omelets, but I'm happy to make whatever you'd like."

Shaun's face brightened. "Actually, I do have a special request. Let me make the omelets for you."

"Oh, no," Melanie protested, "you're our guest. It's my pleasure."

"No, really," Shaun insisted, "I'm not just trying to be nice. I actually love to cook, and I have a secret omelet recipe I've been trying to perfect that I'd love to try out on you. Trust me, it would be *my* pleasure. Please."

Something in Shaun's face and voice persuaded Melanie to give in. She showed their guest around the kitchen, and then she sat on a stool to watch him work.

"How'd you sleep?" Stewart asked as Shaun gathered ingredients.

"Like a baby," Shaun answered. "The bed was wonderful."

As he made the omelets, the Bakers asked him about his family and his work. He shared only the basic details, not yet willing to go too deep. He did reveal the breakup with Amanda, and it was obvious to the Bakers that he wasn't yet over it—not even close. Melanie deftly steered the conversation in another direction.

Shaun soon finished the omelets, delivering them steaming hot on plates. "Okay, fingers crossed . . . ," he said nervously. "Tell me what you think. And be totally honest."

Stewart and Melanie each took a bite. Simultaneously, their expressions melted into ecstasy.

"Oh, my!" Melanie exclaimed. "This is marvelous!"

"Fantastic!" Stewart agreed. "Who knew a simple omelet could be this delicious?"

"Shaun," Melanie said, "You have *got* to tell me how you did this. I wasn't really paying attention to what you were doing as we were talking."

"I normally keep my special recipes a secret," Shaun said, "but since Stewart is sharing his formulas with me, I certainly can reveal one of my formulas."

As he wrote out the recipe, and as Stewart and Melanie continued feasting, Melanie said, "Seriously, Shaun, this is really, really amazing. Have you ever thought of becoming a chef or even opening your own restaurant?"

Shaun laughed and said quickly, "No. Cooking is just a hobby for me." But as he said it, something in Shaun's voice sounded off-key.

After they finished breakfast, Shaun and Stewart went into the library and settled into cushy leather chairs for their first mentoring session.

"All right, Shaun," Stewart began, "let's start with the first law, the Law of Attraction. Ever heard of it?"

Shaun couldn't help rolling his eyes. "Oh, yes. My dad talks about it all the time. To be honest, it really bugs me. I've heard lots of people give it lip service, but I've never seen any of them amount to much. I've always just thought it was psychobabble—mystical mumbo jumbo that charlatans preach to sell books." He caught himself. "I'm sorry. I really am coachable, I swear! I'll just shut up and listen."

Stewart just laughed and said, "I can't say I blame you. The truth is that it really doesn't work for most people. That's why there are *six* laws. The Law of Attraction is almost powerless without the other laws. It sounds great on the surface, and it gets people excited, but unfortunately it's only one piece of a much bigger puzzle, and few people ever understand the full puzzle.

"There may, however, be deeper truths to the Law of Attraction that you don't yet fully understand. I promise you, it will make much more sense once you understand all the laws and you can put the Law of Attraction in its proper context. So for now, just be open to it. Deal?"

"Deal," Shaun reluctantly agreed.

Stewart continued, "Simply put, *the Law of Attraction states that you attract into your life whatever you think about the most. Your dominant and persistent thoughts eventually manifest as physical reality.* As Norman Vincent Peale, who wrote the popular book *The Power of Positive Thinking,* put it, 'The person who sends out positive thoughts activates the world around him positively and draws back to himself positive results.' In other words, what you focus on is what grows.

"Now, this can work either to your benefit or to your destruction. A man who entertains only virtuous, loving thoughts will cultivate a healthy relationship with his spouse. And if a man consistently views pornography and entertains lustful thoughts, I can guarantee that those thoughts will eventually cause him to crash and ruin his marriage. It's inevitable: Thoughts are things, and they manifest as words and often lead to actions. As Ralph Waldo Emerson wrote, 'Sow a thought and you reap an act; sow an act and you reap a habit; sow a habit and you reap a character; sow a character and you reap a destiny.' Shaun, I can't stress this enough: You become what you think.

"The two best books on this law are *Think and Grow Rich* by Napoleon Hill and *As a Man Thinketh* by James Allen. Napoleon Hill teaches that 'our brains become magnetized with the dominating thoughts which we hold in our minds, and by means with which no man is familiar, these "magnets" attract to us the forces, the people, the circumstances of life which harmonize with the nature of our dominating thoughts.'

"James Allen says it more poetically: 'Man is made or unmade by himself; in the armory of thought he forges the weapons by which he destroys himself; he also fashions the tools with which he builds for himself heavenly mansions of joy and strength and peace. By the right choice and true application of thought, man ascends to his Divine Perfection; by the abuse and wrong application of thought, he descends below the level of the beast. Between these two extremes are all the grades of character, and man is their maker and master.'

"Shaun, your thoughts are far more powerful than you've ever understood. Your character is shaped and your achievements are won more by your thoughts than by physical effort. Your success is predicated more on what you *think about* and less on what you *do*, for *what you do* is determined by *how you think*. As Emerson wrote, 'Great men are those who see that thoughts rule the world.'

"No quest in your life is more important than choosing the thoughts you entertain and cultivate. A lifetime of negative thinking will manifest negative results. Likewise, the more positive your thinking, the more positive your results. Successful thinking catalyzes successful actions.

"Shaun, let me ask you a question: What do you want in life?"

"Well, I know I don't want to be a CPA for the next thirty or forty years." Stewart smiled.

"Ah. That's a very predictable answer. But you didn't answer my question. Unfortunately, Shaun, most people manifest more weeds than flowers and fruits, because they focus more on what they *don't* want than on what they *do* want. They're simply not clear on what they want.

"I've asked countless people what they want, and so very many of them start detailing all the things they don't want. For example, they say they don't want to live from paycheck to paycheck. But because that's all they focus on, and they haven't created space and dedicated energy to a higher vision, they continue living from paycheck to paycheck. What they focus on mentally manifests as their reality.

"Shaun, unless you live the Law of Attraction, I can predict where you will be one, five, or even thirty years from now, because you will get exactly what you think about most. If your dominating thought is not wanting to be a CPA, well, you'll stay a CPA while always wishing you were doing something different.

"The challenge is that most people are largely unconscious of their thoughts. Their minds run on autopilot. They simply absorb stimuli from their external environment without really analyzing those stimuli. Not knowing the power of their thoughts, they're careless about what they allow to enter their minds. They passively watch TV and movies, listen to music, surf the Internet, and hang out with negative people—without understanding the impact all of these things have on their lives.

"In this unconscious state, people are essentially powerless to change their reality. They're sleepwalking through life. They're captives of the media and of circumstances. Remember: These six laws are about being a *Conscious Creator*. Elevating your consciousness and being more aware of the power of your thoughts is the first step in the process.

"The more you study and strive to improve, the more you'll realize the truth in the Law of Attraction. I'm not alone in teaching the power of thought. I've quoted already from James Allen, and here's another idea from him: 'You are today where your thoughts have brought you; you will be tomorrow where your thoughts take you.' Albert Einstein said, 'The world we have created is a product of our thinking; it cannot be changed without changing our thinking.'

"Shaun, can you detach from your past negative experiences with this law enough to accept that there is power in your thoughts?"

"Yes," Shaun said. "How you're describing it makes sense. You've made it more real and concrete for me. In the past it has just sounded so . . . mystical."

"Yes, I get it," Stewart acknowledged. "But understanding this law is the starting point of all acts of creation. Everything I have created—my home, my business, my lifestyle, my family, my wealth, my legacy—has all manifested through the Law of Attraction. Anything you want, within natural law, can be yours.

"But understand that the Law of Attraction doesn't have power without the discipline of the other laws. By itself, it's a vehicle without fuel. And that's why it seemed mystical to you: It's incomplete. So let's fuel up the tank, so to speak, by moving on to the Second Law of Conscious Creation.

"This second law gives you the clarity to know what you want, so you can start focusing more on that and less on what you don't want. It is the

Law of Purpose." He paused. "Do you remember the clue we discussed yesterday?"

"Follow your bliss," Shaun responded quickly.

"That's right," Stewart said. "The Law of Purpose is based on three premises: First, that you were born for a specific reason. That there is an innate purpose to your life, unique to you. A calling—or a mission, if you will.

"Second, that your highest potential can be achieved only by aligning with your inborn purpose. That as long as you're ignorant of or resistant to your calling, you will never feel satisfied or perform at full capacity.

"Third, that following your bliss is the doorway to your unique path of purpose. Follow it to pursue those things that give you the highest and purest feelings of joy and satisfaction. Your bliss is like clues placed strategically in your heart by your Creator. As you follow the trail of clues, not only do you become happy, but you also serve others better.

"*The Law of Purpose states that for you to achieve your highest potential, your desires and actions must be manifestations of your True Self and True Purpose.* Your True Self is who you really are at your highest and deepest spiritual core, beyond ego, vice, and self-deception. The you who does things because they are right, regardless of consequence . . . who seeks lasting joy over fleeting pleasure . . . who thinks bigger than yourself and wants more than to simply elevate yourself in the eyes of others. It is your intuition whispering to you through the shouting of crowds. Your True Self is your conscience; it gives you satisfaction when you do right and distress when you stray off your right path.

"Your True Purpose, then, is your True Self in action. It is manifested by the things that come naturally to you . . . the things that make you lose all sense of time doing them . . . the things you would do even if you never got paid a dime or if no one ever noticed . . . the things you can't not do, because they are so compelling and irresistible to you. It is who you were born to become. Your exclusive combination of passions, gifts, talents, values, knowledge, and curiosity, all colliding into a divine focal point, a world-changing mission.

"Simply put, this second law says you need to know who you truly are and what you were born to do, and you need to follow that knowledge with commitment and integrity. See, the Law of Attraction can't work for your benefit until you actually know who you are and what you want. Until you know your purpose, you're stuck wandering through life, bellyaching about what you *don't* want.

"Andrew Carnegie powerfully explained the relationship between the Law of Attraction and the Law of Purpose when he said, 'When a person adopts a definite purpose in life, forms a definite plan for attaining it, and brings this purpose and plan into his mind many times daily—fanning it into a white flame of enthusiasm as he lives it out step by step—he forms a definite thought habit which goes right on working while he sleeps, the same as when he is awake. By this means one may condition his subconscious mind to aid him in circumventing his lack of formal education, and aid him in the solution of seemingly insurmountable obstacles.'

"Notice that the Law of Purpose encompasses both knowing and doing. You can't align with your True Self if you don't know who you are. And once you do know who you are and what you were born for, you have a sacred obligation to act on that knowledge."

"Wait a second," Shaun interrupted. "I'm confused. Isn't it redundant to say that I have to align with myself? I mean, how can I ever *not* be aligned with myself, because I am *me*, am I not?" He paused. "Does that make any sense?"

Stewart smiled enigmatically. "Haven't you ever felt yourself competing with yourself? Haven't you been drawn to and tempted by things you know can't lead to anything good? Haven't you felt that internal struggle between the high road and the comfortable road?"

Shaun thought for a moment, then nodded. "I guess you're right. I *have* felt that. In fact, it's why I'm sitting here now. It's almost like there are two versions of myself competing with each other. And I'm sad to say that in my life, I don't think the best man has usually won."

"It's not 'almost' like that," Stewart responded. "It's *exactly* like that. That is the essence of human nature. You are two selves: your false, ego self and your true, spiritual self. For the sake of simplicity, think of it as a lower and a higher self. Or, as I like to call them, the Victim and the Victor. The goal of the six laws is to overcome the Victim and live as a Victor.

"There's a story that teaches this concept well. In 1957, a Buddhist monastery in Thailand was being relocated. Along with everything else, a giant clay statue of Buddha had to be moved. While the monks were moving it, one of them noticed a crack in the statue. Concerned about damaging the statue, they decided to wait a day before continuing the move.

"During the night, one of the monks checked on the statue, shining his flashlight over the entire Buddha. When his light swept over the crack, a glimmer of light reflected back at him. Curious, the monk got a hammer and chisel and chipped away the clay. As he knocked off piece after piece of clay, the Buddha got brighter and brighter. After hours of work, the monk was astounded to realize that the entire statue was solid gold.

"Historians believe the Buddha had been covered with clay by monks several hundred years earlier, before an attack by the Burmese army. The monks had covered the Buddha to protect it. All the monks were killed in the attack, however, so it wasn't until 1957 that the great treasure was discovered.

"Your lower self is like this outer shell of clay, hiding your true, radiant self from the world. Your task is to chip away this lower self, or Victim, to reveal your brilliance as a Victor.

"Your inner Victim tends toward selfishness, greed, and pride and is motivated more by fear than by love, passion, or anything else. It cares less about seeking and aligning with truth than it cares about being right. It often settles for temporary pleasure at the expense of lasting happiness.

"In most people the Victim manifests as mere mediocrity. It seeks the path of least resistance. It wants comfort and security, not greatness. And ironically, even though all it cares about is its own security and happiness, it can never achieve them; these things are eternally lost to the person. That's why those stuck in the lower self often play the Victim. They always have someone or some circumstance to blame for the bad things that happen to them. As long as they have someone else to blame, they don't have to face the hard reality about themselves. They justify their failures with excuses.

"I saw an MSNBC report that said eighty-seven percent of Americans don't like their jobs. That statistic was staggering enough. But what really baffled me was when an 'expert' said in the report that 'most of us just can't quit our jobs.' Here we are in the freest, most prosperous country in the history of the world, yet so many people still speak the language of slaves. The truth is that most people *won't* quit their jobs because they're too stuck in their comfort zone, and getting out of it is too scary.

"Now, there's really nothing intrinsically wrong with the desire for comfort and security. The trick is learning to put it in its proper context so you can dream beyond the mediocrity it so often leads to.

"I met a guy once who had worked for an airline for twenty-two years. He said he hated his job, but if he worked there for three more years, he'd get flight benefits. His employer wasn't even offering a pension. I was stunned. He'd already worked twenty-two years doing something he hated, and he was prepared to sacrifice the next three years of his life, often being away from his family, being totally unhappy, just so he could get a few free flights?

"Again, comfort, security, and such benefits as employer-paid health insurance are nice. But are they really the most important things in life? Should they be your highest aspiration?

"Now, in contrast to this lower, fearful self," Stewart continued, "your higher self is your internal Victor. It's the hero in you and inside every one of us. Your inner Victor rises above injuries, heartaches, and trials. In fact, troubles make the Victor stronger. The Victor takes ultimate responsibility for your life's results, for your attitude, for your responses to even the most tragic circumstances.

"The Victor yearns for greatness, to create, to build, to achieve, to leave a legacy. And it's precisely because the Victor sees beyond comfort and security that the Victor is able to achieve the highest, truest, most sustainable levels of comfort and security. When you live from your highest self, you have ultimate confidence in your ability to transcend circumstances—to produce your way out of any temporary failure. When you operate from your higher self, you have power to collaborate with the universe in the miracle of creation.

"Your inner Victor will never seek its own happiness to the detriment of others. It seeks to serve, uplift, and bless the lives of others. It wants everyone to experience true happiness. It sees through the illusions of vice, the paths that can lead to sorrow and addiction. It strives to align its thoughts, speech, and actions with truth. It lives from faith, not fear.

"But isn't there a healthy purpose for fear?" Shaun interjected.

"Explain," Stewart replied.

"Well," Shaun said, "my deepest fear, which has driven everything I've done since leaving college, has been that I'll turn out like my father. When you talk about these deep, inspirational things, you stir passion inside me. But

I always feel myself holding back, because my dad used to talk like this too. And even though I love him deeply, to be honest he's never really amounted to much. He's spent his whole life chasing dreams. And it seems as if those dreams change from day to day.

"My dad never really stuck with any one thing. We moved around a lot because he took a lot of different jobs. He never earned a lot of money, so I grew up poor and I hated it. And I can't even count the number of network marketing companies he's joined. Of course, he was going to 'hit it big' with every one, but he fizzled out almost as soon as he joined them.

"It's why I became a CPA. I saw the contrast between my father and my uncle Frank, who was a CPA with the same company for forty years. My uncle has enjoyed a comfortable, stable, secure life. He's even what I'd call 'rich.' His kids always wore nice clothes and had great Christmases. Growing up, I envied them. I know being a CPA isn't what I was born to do, but at least it's better than what my father has done. So I feel as though that fear is what has driven me here today."

Stewart nodded. "Yes, I know what you mean, and I can see how that would create confusion for you. I can see why you made the choices you have. But keep in mind that you're here for a reason. That fear may have gotten you a college degree and a job, but you're obviously dissatisfied, right?"

Shaun acknowledged this with a nod.

Stewart continued, "There are counterfeits of everything. Fear can be effective as a temporary motivator, but it's a counterfeit of the deep desire that comes from knowing who you are and what you were born to accomplish.

"Likewise, comfort and security can be counterfeits. Like I said, they aren't necessarily bad things in and of themselves. In fact, they're natural by-products of living as a Conscious Creator. But as I mentioned earlier, their counterfeit is a safe but fear-based mediocrity. When they become your primary pursuit—as opposed to the greatness of creation—you lose sight of bigger and better things.

"On the other hand, there's a counterfeit to living your dreams that's more talk than action. It's flightiness. Surfing on the ocean of life, in search of that next big wave that's going to launch you onto the fantasy island of selfish prosperity, is a counterfeit for actually achieving your dreams. I can't comment on your father specifically without knowing him, but I have met a lot of people like this.

"In contrast to both of these counterfeits, True Purpose is a fixed, immovable North Star. It lifts your vision to greater things than comfort and security. It gives you the strength, determination, and direction to navigate through the winds and waves of changing circumstances. Conscious Creators are not drifters or surfers on the ocean of life. They are sailors—or 'navigators,' as author Roy H. Williams puts it.

"The truth is that the phrase 'Follow your bliss' is misleading for many people. Just because a certain path brings you bliss doesn't mean it's easy. In fact, the people throughout history who have followed their bliss the most passionately are often those who experienced hardships—George Washington, Joan of Arc, Martin Luther King, Jr., Gandhi."

Stewart pulled another book from the bookshelf. "Yesterday I quoted from Joseph Campbell about how he created that phrase," he said. "There's another passage from the same book that can give you even more insight. It says:

When I taught in a boys' prep school, I used to talk to the boys who were trying to make up their minds as to what their careers were going to be. A boy would come to me and ask, 'Do you think I can do this? Do you think I can do that? Do you think I can be a writer?

'Oh,' I would say, 'I don't know. Can you endure ten years of disappointment with nobody responding to you, or are you thinking that you are going to write a bestseller the first crack? If you have the guts to stay with the thing you really want, no matter what happens, well, go ahead.'

"In other words," Stewart said, "following your bliss is no picnic, necessarily. The path isn't paved with gold. Your bank account won't always be overflowing, your pantry may not always be full. In fact, in some ways this path of bliss, purpose, and creation is harder than selling out to comfort and security. But there is one guarantee: When you stick it out, it will be worth it. It's fulfilling beyond anything imagined by those wallowing in mediocrity.

"Too often we see just the final product of successful people; we don't see the journey they took to get there. You see my house and property now, but you didn't experience the times when Melanie and I ate Top Ramen for months and sat on Salvation Army furniture for years because we were sacrificing to build our business. You didn't see me lying down and pounding on the floor in frustration when my first business failed and I was forced into bankruptcy. You didn't help me make the agonizing decisions of whom to let go when my second business started floundering. You didn't see me go through the humiliating process of begging my bankers for mercy.

"So because they see the fruits of success without understanding the process of sacrifice and cultivation, people develop an entitlement mentality. They want it all, they want it now, and they think the world owes it all to them. Young married couples go into debt because they want now what it took their parents years to build. People vote for politicians based on who will give them the most government benefits. They want shortcuts and quick fixes for everything. They treat their bodies horribly and eat convenient, processed junk, and then they want pills and liposuction to repair the damage. They develop a something-for-nothing attitude; they think that wealth and success are the products of luck.

"Following your bliss and living from your True Self and for your True Purpose—it's hard work. But when you have that clarity and drive, you're willing to do what it takes. And despite any challenges, it's more satisfying than I can describe—not just the end result, but also the process, the journey. And when you do stick with it, you find that following your bliss leads to discovering your purpose—and as you live your purpose, you experience greater bliss. In other words, the perseverance creates a self-reinforcing cycle. But you can't give up."

Stewart paused to let his words sink in.

Though Shaun felt a bit overwhelmed by it all, what Stewart was saying resonated deeply with him. But he wasn't about to blindly accept anything either. He chewed on what he'd heard for a moment. Then he said, "It all makes sense. But I'm still trying to figure out why I have such a hard time feeling and recognizing my bliss. I can tell you things I enjoy, but I guess I don't have the confidence to know which things I should really devote my life to."

Stewart answered, "That speaks to a critical component of learning and living this first law, the Law of Attraction: You need to engage outside help—mentors, family, friends—who can see you more objectively than you may see yourself. Introspection is critical too, but sometimes a wise mentor makes all the difference." He paused. "I bet you've heard the phrase 'Know thyself.'"

"Sure," Shaun said.

"But do you know where it comes from?" Stewart asked.

"Not really."

"According to the ancient Greek writer Pausanias, *'gnothi seauton,'* meaning 'know thyself,' was inscribed in the forecourt of the Temple of Apollo at Delphi. The concept was fundamental to the Greeks, and it meant multiple things to them. For one, it was a proverb intended to make people humble—to keep them from boasting or thinking more about themselves than was merited. It was an admonition to remember your place in relationship to your Creator. It was also a piece of advice saying that you should trust your thoughts over the opinions of crowds.

"Many wise men through the ages have commented on the concept. Benjamin Franklin admitted how hard it was to apply this advice, when he wrote, 'There are three things extremely hard: steel, a diamond, and to know one's self.'

"I can attest to that," Stewart continued. "It hasn't been easy for me to learn myself deeply enough to really live this law, but I've had mentors along the way to help me see things I was too stuck inside my own box to see.

"When we're done today, remind me to give you an exercise that will help you uncover your bliss and develop a clear purpose."

"I'm excited to hear more about that exercise," said Shaun. Ever cautious and methodical, however, he was still trying to find loopholes and weaknesses in the first two laws. "But isn't this all kind of selfish? How can I be sure that what I want is what my Creator wants for me? How can I know that it's what serves a higher good rather than simply making me feel good in the moment?"

"Good question," Stewart said. "Emerson wrote a poem called 'Gnothi Seauton' that I believe answers it. It's a deep poem, and I highly recommend that you study and memorize it. He essentially says you can know when you're doing right by getting in touch with your higher self, or as he says it, 'God dwells in thee.' You can think of this higher self as your conscience. It takes time, effort, and discernment to recognize it, but it's there, and you'll feel it. And as you learn to trust and follow it, you'll know when you're doing the right things.

"Now, I certainly understand that pursuing one's own pleasure can be selfish. But the fact that something makes you personally happy doesn't make it a selfish pursuit by default. Why would your Creator plant seeds in your soul that bring you joy and then expect you to stifle them?

"The key is in differentiating between the desires of your lower self and those of your higher self. To be in tune with your higher self is to be in tune with divinity. In other words, when you're acting from your higher self, you can be one hundred percent confident that your desires are aligned with those of your Creator. For example, name an activity you enjoy."

"Well," Shaun said, "I like mountain biking."

"Well, if you feel a deep and abiding calling to ride mountain bikes, then by all means, do it. Now, if you were to spend the rest of your life mountain biking because it were purely a selfish desire of your lower self, an escape from responsibility, it would be a tragic waste of your life. But if mountain biking—or whatever else it may be—is your True Purpose, I guarantee it would both bring you joy as well as serve humanity in some way."

"I can see that," Shaun said. "And I can also see how critical it is to really be in tune with myself and to want things for the right reasons."

"That's absolutely right," Stewart said. "To live this second law requires that you align your desires correctly. And for most people this means a dramatic realignment. Your desires are either in alignment with your True Self and True Purpose or in alignment with your lower self, your ego. Anyone can accumulate wealth or achieve fame, but if they're doing it for their ego, they'll never be satisfied. Misaligned desires lead to destruction and heartache. I know people who sacrificed everything, including their families and closest relationships, to pursue fame and fortune. And in the end their families were torn apart and they were miserable.

"But when you do the right things for the right reasons, the windows of heaven open and you find yourself wealthier than you ever imagined. And speaking of which, you'll also learn to define wealth accurately. It's tragic to me how many people spend their lives pursuing money. The truth is that no one actually wants money. What people want is satisfaction, fulfillment, peace, happiness. They think money will give them those things. Money is certainly one component of wealth, but the truly wealthy people are those who have found and are living their mission, regardless of how much money it earns them.

"But here's the really cool part: Nothing gives you a greater chance of creating and enjoying material abundance in your life than following your bliss, even if you can't immediately see how the things you love to do could be used to make money. Does everyone who follows their bliss become a millionaire? Of course not. But you have a much greater chance of prospering when you do what you love and let the money follow, rather than sacrificing your bliss to go after money."

"After how I was raised," Shaun said, "it's a tough concept for me to swallow. I became a CPA so I could earn steady income, to never worry about money. And I've saved diligently and tried to be wise with my money. As a child I experienced the lack of money, and I never want to experience it again."

"I'm not telling you money's not important or to pay no attention to it," Stewart said. "I'm simply saying you have to put it in its proper context. The point is to focus on purpose, not money. Your purpose should determine how you earn and use your money, rather than money determining your life decisions and overshadowing your purpose.

"And speaking of purpose, part of mine is that my family comes first, and I've got to get my son to a soccer game. Have I given you enough to work with?"

"Oh, more than enough," Shaun said. "You've been so generous. I can't thank you enough. I definitely see how this is going to be life-changing for me. I think it will take a while to sink in, but I know I'll be making some changes."

Stewart stood and shook his hand. "I'm happy to be of service. Go home and ponder the Law of Attraction and the Law of Purpose. Try to get in touch with your True Self and identify your bliss. If you need any help along the way, feel free to e-mail me or even call me." He took a business card out of his wallet and handed it to Shaun. "And when you have achieved clarity about yourself and your purpose, we'll proceed to the next law."

"You mentioned some exercise you use," Shaun said. "Can I get that before I leave?"

"Oh, the Purpose Finder—I'm glad you reminded me," Stewart said. He retrieved a piece of paper from his desk, gave it to Shaun, and wished him luck.

As Shaun was leaving, Melanie caught him and handed him lunch in a bag. "Thanks again for those amazing omelets this morning. And for giving me the recipe. I guarantee I'll be using it often."

"Oh no, thank *you*," Shaun said. "I had fun cooking for you. And Stewart has given me plenty of food for thought. I've had a wonderful time here."

He walked to his car, lost in thought. Before leaving, he sat in the driver's seat and read the questions on the Purpose Finder exercise, and then he pondered them on the long drive home.

* * *

Readers: *The Conscious Creator's Reparadigming Journal,* which accompanies this book, has a series of powerful exercises to help you through this entire process—including the Purpose Finder exercise that will help you find and define your purpose. Download a digital copy for free or order a hard copy at www.ConsciousCreatorBook.com. Your experience with this book is incomplete without it.

So far, Stewart has taught Shaun two of the Six Laws of Conscious Creation. They are:

The First Law of Conscious Creation: The Law of Attraction

You attract into your life whatever you think about the most. Your dominant and persistent thoughts eventually manifest as physical reality.

The Second Law of Conscious Creation: The Law of Purpose

For you to achieve your highest potential, your desires and actions must be manifestations of your True Self and True Purpose. Your True Self embodies the highest, most accurate truth from which you can create at your greatest potential. Conscious Creators know who they are and what they were born to accomplish.

SIX

Monday morning found Shaun at his desk once more, happy but distracted. He had arrived home from Stewart's house late Saturday night and had spent all Sunday completing Stewart's Purpose Finder exercise. It required deep introspection and honesty. He was enjoying the process, though, pondering things he hadn't thought about for years.

Many of Shaun's answers surprised him, since he'd been so unconscious of the subject matter dealt with by the questions. And while he did feel good about his answers, he also felt fearful about their implications—what it would mean to his life and career if he were to go in the directions that his answers indicated.

He was also struggling with putting all the pieces together into a coherent focal point, or what Stewart had called a "North Star." Shaun was starting to get some sense of his purpose, but he wasn't quite sure how it could be expressed in a way that would make financial sense.

Furthermore, he was still debating with himself over how much merit there was to this whole *Follow your bliss* idea. Was it universal, or was it simply one way of looking at life that happened to work for Stewart? He decided to get a second opinion from his uncle Frank, the retired CPA, who lived in nearby Tempe. He called Frank and arranged a visit for the next evening.

At Frank's place, his wife, Cathy, greeted Shaun at the door with a hug.

"Come on in, Shaun," she said, ushering him to the living room, where Frank was watching golf on TV.

Frank switched off the TV and stood to greet Shaun. "Hey, Shaun," he boomed, "how's my favorite CPA?"

"Well," Shaun said, "personally I'm doing just fine. But the CPA part of me isn't doing so fine. That's what I wanted to talk to you about."

"Have a seat," Frank said as Cathy brought in a plate of cookies, then left. "What's on your mind?" he asked. "I don't know that I'll have any answers for you, but I'll give it a shot."

Shaun began, "You knew my girlfriend, Amanda, right?"

"Yes . . . ," Frank said.

"Well, she broke up with me a while ago."

"I'm sorry to hear that," Frank said sympathetically. "Cathy and I thought you two seemed like the perfect match."

"That's what I thought, too," said Shaun. "But I guess I just wasn't right for her. And the truth is, what hurts the most is that I think she's right about some things. Ever since she broke up with me, I've been questioning a lot of things about my life. I met an interesting man named Stewart Baker, who has shared some ideas with me about how to live with purpose and conviction. I find his ideas fascinating, but I've always looked up to you and wanted to get your opinion. You're the reason I became a CPA.

"No disrespect to Dad, but I always envied you and your family growing up. You've just always seemed like you had it all together, like you had a plan and you followed it through. I've tried to follow your example, but I'm missing something. I had my life all planned out, but things have changed now. I know I won't be able to stick with the plan, so now I'm wondering where that leaves me."

"I'm flattered," Frank said, "but I never thought I was anyone to look up to. I've simply enjoyed my life and tried to be a good person."

"Well, that's actually right in line with what I wanted to ask you," Shaun said. He explained everything he knew about being a Conscious Creator—about the Law of Attraction and the Law of Purpose, the concept of following one's bliss.

"So what do you think?" Shaun asked. "Is Stewart on to something I should listen to, or is this just one way of looking at life?"

Frank's answer startled Shaun. "I couldn't agree with him more. Following your bliss is the only way to live."

"But wait a second," Shaun protested. "I'm confused. I've always thought you chose your career for the money and security. And don't get me wrong; I always looked at that as a good thing, as the smart way to live."

"Well," Frank answered, "I can't say I didn't appreciate the money and security. But that's not why I did it. The truth is that I really loved accounting and being a CPA, and I was darn good at it. How else do you think I stuck with it for forty years? Cathy had to practically beg me to retire, and I could have retired much sooner than I did. But I was enjoying myself too much. There's just something about numbers and ledgers and balance sheets that really jazzes me. You know your father and I used to work in your grandfather's department store, right?"

"Of course," Shaun said, "I've heard plenty of stories."

"But did you know I used to handle all the bookkeeping?" Frank asked.

"No, I didn't," Shaun said.

"Your grandfather taught me how to do it, and within a few months I was giving him insights about the company that he'd never considered.

He made me the official bookkeeper and started growing the store with my ideas, and that was the start of my accounting career. There are plenty of people much smarter than me in other ways. I've done accounting for plenty of entrepreneurs who were much more talented and made way more money than me. But where they're able to create something out of thin air, I'm better at working with things on a more concrete level. I love discovering the truth that numbers can reveal. I'm a big believer in hard data, and that's what numbers give you. See, I'm not any more responsible or wise than your father. I was just lucky enough to find something I loved."

"But what if what you love doing doesn't bring you security or doesn't make much money?" Shaun asked.

"I can't answer that question for everyone," Frank said, "but for me, no amount of money or security is worth wasting life on something you don't enjoy. Those things are nice, but they're way overrated relative to your ultimate happiness. Sure, they can contribute to happiness, but doing what you love is a much more important factor. And considering the people I've known throughout my life, I can say confidently that when you do what you love, those other things have a way of working out on their own. Not everyone I've known who loved what they did became superrich, but they always got along just fine. And their happiness more than compensated for their not being rich."

Hearing this from a man he looked up to was exactly what Shaun needed to commit fully to following his bliss. He drove home, deep in thought and ready to make some changes.

The next morning Shaun decided he should try to improve things in his job before trying to implement other ideas that had been sparked while completing the exercise. He thought this would be the smart way to ease into this new path of bliss without much risk.

He spent the next week brainstorming ideas about what he could change within his job to enjoy it more while bringing more value to clients of his firm. He found that he was actually quite innovative—much more so than he'd ever displayed for Amanda or anyone at work. He'd simply been stifling his innovative spirit. He also found that once he'd turned on his idea machine, it was hard to turn it off. The ideas were coming so fast and furious, it felt like a treasure chest had been unlocked in his soul. His ideas often woke him up in the middle of the night, and after losing a particularly good idea by going back to sleep one night, he started getting up and writing down his best nocturnal insights.

At first Shaun's ideas were so expansive that they had little practical value. But over time he was able to rein them in and make them more applicable. He kept a notebook, where he mapped out each idea and performed financial calculations on its potential effect.

Shaun was brimming with ideas for one client in particular, a restaurant owner. He decided to limit his presentation to that one client. If that worked, his firm could apply his ideas to more clients. Shaun finally felt comfortable with his plan and was ready to present it to his boss, Ryan.

He scheduled a meeting with Ryan and fine-tuned his presentation. He showed up for the meeting in his best suit, fully prepared with a PowerPoint presentation and a folder with detailed charts and graphs.

"Come on in," Ryan said in a tired and somber tone that rang alarm bells in Shaun's unconscious mind. "How can I help you?" Disregarding the subconscious warning, Shaun plunged into his presentation. "I've been thinking a lot about my job lately. The truth is that I'm just not inspired by it. I know you're probably not used to hearing this from employees, but I want to be completely honest with you so I can perform better for you. I have some ideas of how I'd like to change my position so I'll enjoy it more and to create more value for our clients."

Shaun shared his ideas, using his printouts to back up specific concepts. Lost in the possibilities, his excitement increased the longer he talked.

Suddenly, Ryan raised his hand. "Shaun, I'm sorry, but I'm going to stop you right there. I don't have time to get into this right now."

Shaun halted, deflated and confused. He'd expected the ideas to be so compelling that he'd practically win awards for them.

Ryan continued wearily, "The hard truth is this: I've been asked by corporate to get rid of five people from our office. This isn't easy for me, but the fact that you just told me you don't enjoy your job made the decision for me. Everything you've outlined sounds great, but it's not really what we do. I need someone who can do what's asked without getting bored. I'm sorry, but I'm going to have to let you go. Effective immediately."

SEVEN

Crushed, Shaun shuffled out of Ryan's office. This was the last thing he had expected. *I get fired for trying to improve the company?* he thought. *Incredible. This is how I get rewarded for innovating? So much for following my bliss.*

He spent the next couple days on the couch, numb and listless. The devastating combination of Amanda throwing him over and being fired left him completely uprooted and unsure of himself. Thankfully, like a good accountant, he'd been saving fifteen percent of his income since starting his job, so he had a comfortable financial buffer. The company's severance package would also help. Still, being blindsided was a severe blow. Despite completing his Purpose Finder exercise, he had no idea what to do next. He was used to doors opening for him, not closing behind him.

As Shaun wallowed in self-pity, the numbness turned into bitterness. Hadn't he always done the right things? Hadn't he tried to be a good person? Didn't he *deserve* better than this? The bitterness turned into blame as his brain scrambled for an explanation. If Amanda hadn't dumped him, none of this would have happened. If Stewart hadn't filled his head with all that passion, purpose, and attraction crap, he'd be okay. He'd been doing just fine without it, thank you very much. He shouldn't have gotten his hopes up and let his guard down. He should have just swallowed his discontentment at work and stuck with his life's plan.

Feeling defeated, he was thoroughly unmotivated to move forward. He tried picking up a few of the books he'd bought before meeting Stewart, but he couldn't get into them. He made a light effort to peruse online job boards, but after two weeks, still nothing interested him. He forced himself to go hiking and mountain biking occasionally, but his heart wasn't in it and he usually cut his outings short. His mother called him frequently, but he never felt like returning her calls. At her urging, he did have Sunday dinners at his parents' house as usual, but he was distant and despondent.

There was one place where he always found solace: the kitchen. Cooking was the one thing he looked forward to, the only habit he didn't shelve. With all this time on his hands, exploring specialty food shops became his getaway as he experimented with new dishes.

Shaun arrived home from shopping one afternoon to find his mother's car in his driveway. *Great,* he thought, *here comes the lecture.* He'd always had a great relationship with his mother. She was the responsible and grounded one in her marriage, and he had always appreciated that and been drawn to her because of it. But it was precisely her emphasis on responsibility that, by not returning her calls, he had been trying to avoid.

He parked, grabbed his bags, and approached her car as she stepped out.

"Hi, Shaun!" she called, trying to sound cheerful.

"Hey, Mom. It's good to see you," Shaun lied, as he gave her a hug. "Come on in."

"I can't stay long," she said as she sat down in a chair in the living room. "I just wanted to say one thing, and then I'll leave you alone. Listen, I know why you haven't been returning my calls, and it's okay. I know this is a tough time for you and you just need some time to sort things out. I promise, I don't want to lecture you. I trust you and know you'll make the right decisions."

"Thanks, Mom," Shaun said, still feeling slightly defensive.

She continued, "I know how it feels to be let down when you think you're doing the right things. When I had my miscarriage before you were born, I was devastated. I wanted children so badly. Everything had been going so well, and then my heart was broken. I spent a few weeks depressed and angry. I blamed God. I blamed the doctors. I even blamed myself. But a wise friend helped me come out of it by taking me to the women's shelter where she volunteered. We went two or three times a week, and it was seeing the pain and feeling the heartache of those other women that helped me to see beyond my self-pity and gave me the courage to try again. I don't blame you for how you feel. Doing volunteer work helped me, and I just wanted to gently suggest that you find a place to volunteer. Anything where you can help other people. Just think about it, will you?"

"Sure, Mom," Shaun said, without much conviction. "I'll try."

She stood, hugged him and kissed him on the cheek. "See you Sunday afternoon?"

"Yes," he sighed, "I'll be there."

Shaun processed his mother's advice as he cooked dinner. The problem was that holding on to the anger, hurt, and blame felt strangely satisfying, and he wasn't quite ready to let it go. Deep down, and however twisted, he knew it gave him an explanation for not succeeding. He told himself he'd take an opportunity to volunteer if it came up, but he wasn't yet committed to actively seeking it out.

As he cooked, he glanced out the kitchen window and saw a Meals on Wheels delivery truck pull up to the curb in front of his neighbor's house. Dorothy's husband had died a year earlier, and although her family had urged her to move into a retirement home, she wasn't ready to leave the house she'd lived in with her husband for thirty-five years. Shaun occasionally helped her around the house, and he enjoyed visiting with her. Seeing the delivery truck now, he was reminded that Dorothy had asked him to change a lightbulb for her.

He dried his hands and walked across the street to her house, catching her just as the deliveryman was leaving. "Hey, Dorothy," he said, "is now a good time for me to change that lightbulb?"

"Oh, sure," she said, opening the screen door. "I've got bulbs in the pantry."

He followed her as she walked slowly and painfully into a back bedroom, using her walker.

"That's the one," she pointed.

Shaun changed the bulb and then walked down the hall to where he found Dorothy sitting at the dining room table, opening her meal containers.

"Meat loaf and fake mashed potatoes again," she said. "I wish I had the strength and energy to cook like I used to. Dale loved my mashed potatoes, and I guarantee you, I never used that powdered junk."

"Do your kids ever cook for you?" Shaun asked.

"Well, for Thanksgiving and Christmas, but that's about it," she said. "But that doesn't matter much to me. What I really wish is that they'd just come see me more often. I know they're all busy with their own lives, but I sure get lonely here."

Shaun was suddenly struck with an idea. "Dorothy, I've got a favor to ask you. I've been trying a new shrimp linguini recipe tonight, and I'm just about done cooking. Would you save your meat loaf for tomorrow and try my linguini instead? I really need a second opinion."

"You don't have to tell me twice!" she exclaimed. "Shrimp is one of my favorites. Dale and I used to love going to Red Lobster, and I always loaded up on shrimp."

"Excellent. Give me fifteen minutes and I'll be back over."

Shaun rushed back to his house to finish the meal, then packaged it and took it over to Dorothy's house.

"Now, you've got to promise me to be honest," he said, dishing her up some pasta, tossed salad, and garlic bread. "You won't hurt my feelings if you don't like it."

Dorothy took a bite and chewed thoughtfully. Her eyes closed in pleasure. "Oh, my. Now that is *real* cooking. This is heavenly! Shaun, I had no idea you were such a great chef. I thought you did something with numbers, but surely you must work at a restaurant."

Shaun laughed. "Actually, I don't work anywhere right now. I was fired from my job two weeks ago. I was an accountant. I've never been a chef. I do love cooking, but it's just a hobby for me."

"Well, why on earth have you never considered being a chef?" Dorothy asked. "People would pay good money for your marvelous cooking."

"I guess I never really thought about it," Shaun said. "I just had my sights set on other goals. But to tell you the truth, I did start thinking recently, about a week before I lost my job, about making a change. I don't have anything figured out yet, but who knows? Maybe I will become a chef." He paused. "I'll tell you what: How about you become my first victim? I've got plenty of time on my hands while I'm looking for another job. I think I can give Meals on Wheels a run for its money."

"After tasting this, I wouldn't turn that offer down in a million years," Dorothy said. "Of course, I don't want you to feel obligated, but this is just too good to pass up."

"It's official, then," Shaun said. "Any special requests?"

"Well, now that you mention it, if it's not too much trouble, I have been aching for chicken cordon bleu."

"You've got a deal. Chicken cordon bleu is on the menu for tomorrow night," Shaun announced, even though he considered chicken cordon bleu a little too ordinary to be part of his usual repertoire. But he decided he would start Dorothy out with just what she asked for.

Back home, Shaun realized he hadn't been thinking about his own problems through the whole meal, which he and Dorothy had shared. Feeling good, he called his mom's cell phone. She didn't answer, so he left a quick message: "Mom, I just wanted to tell you that you were right. Thanks for stopping by today. I love you."

For the next week, he pampered Dorothy every evening with one gourmet meal after another. He ate every dinner with her and thoroughly enjoyed the time they spent together. He never tired of watching Dorothy's reaction upon taking the first bite of a new dish. *I could get used to this,* he thought.

Shaun's self-pity and bitterness melted. He still felt confused by the turn of events after trying to follow his bliss, but he stopped blaming Stewart. In fact, he decided to get in touch with Stewart, so he e-mailed him and scheduled a phone call. It was time for new insights.

EIGHT

"Well, have you discovered your purpose yet?" came Stewart's first question when Shaun called.

"Not quite," Shaun said. "In fact, I feel like I'm further away from it. I did complete the Purpose Finder exercise. It was hard, and I don't feel entirely settled on a lot of things, but I enjoyed it. It sparked tons of ideas for me." He paused. "But I got fired."

"Is that a bad thing?" Stewart asked innocently.

"What do you mean?" Shaun blurted. "How could it possibly be a good thing? It's horrible! And it certainly wasn't what I expected from following my bliss. Call me naïve, but I thought that following my bliss would make life easier."

"How do you know it hasn't?" Stewart asked gently, in typical guru fashion.

"Losing my job isn't exactly my idea of an easy life," Shaun said. He gave Stewart the details of what had happened at work. "So instead of opening doors for me, I feel like all it did was close doors."

"Ah," Stewart said, "but closed doors are often far more valuable than open doors. Shaun, you've just been given a profound gift: the opportunity to get closer to who you were meant to become. A path has closed to you, and life has invited you to consider others. You've told me yourself that you know being a CPA isn't your true calling. Well, you've just been nudged off that path. So where's the loss?"

"Well, there's the loss of income for one," Shaun said, still holding on to his frustration. "Not to mention all the lost years and money I spent on school if I don't stick with an accounting career."

"But have those truly been a loss in your life?" Stewart pressed. "Have you not learned anything through the process? Was that college education not valuable? You must have taken a lot of courses that weren't accounting courses. And surely those enriched your life.

"What you call a loss, I call progress. Of course, it *is* a loss if all you see in getting fired is negativity. And, of course, as we learn from the Law of Attraction, negativity attracts more negativity—until you're consumed by it.

"Doors closing and perceived setbacks are both guideposts and tests. They reveal your false and limiting beliefs. They help you identify your blocks. As you strive to follow your bliss, it's inevitable that you experience opposition. And opposition is good for you, because you gain power as you overcome obstacles by staying committed to the process of following your bliss. Speaking of which, notice the word 'following' in that phrase. You may never *arrive* at some point of ultimate bliss, a nirvana where every single thing in your life is perfect. It's a process, a journey. And as long as you keep moving forward, your time, money, and effort are never lost."

"Okay, I guess I see your point," Shaun said. "But it's hard to get excited about this so-called progress when a new path hasn't opened for me yet. I still feel like I'm in the dark."

"I understand," Stewart said. "I've been there too. But I want you to consider a different perspective on loss. You've told me that you know you weren't born to be a CPA. Well, suppose you were to continue down that path. Yes, you could earn a living and probably find a measure of happiness. But what about what you *could have done* with your life instead? What if there's something deep inside you waiting to emerge, something wonderful and world-changing?

"Well, I know there is something like that inside you, because it's inside everyone, and because I've felt your personal greatness. And if you were to continue down this path that bores you, that doesn't represent your passions and purpose, what a tragic loss! The world would never receive your true gifts. That's the only loss worth losing sleep over. With the right attitude, any other perceived loss is simply a lesson learned, a step closer to your true path."

Shaun was quiet for a moment. "It makes sense," he said finally. "But where do I go from here? I've tried looking for other jobs, and nothing really interests me. I even considered a few accounting positions, but I just haven't felt motivated to pursue them."

"Has there been nothing at all that has interested you over the past few weeks?" Stewart asked.

"Not really," Shaun said. Then he thought a moment. "Well, there is one thing. I have an elderly neighbor whose husband died a year ago. One day I saw Meals on Wheels show up at her house, and I knew I could cook something better for her. So I've been cooking dinner for her every night. I've really been enjoying it. But I can't imagine it's the doorway to anything particularly special."

"That's wonderful!" Stewart said. "And why in the world would you not consider it to be a clue leading you in the right direction?"

"I don't know," Shaun said. "I guess I've just never considered cooking for old ladies to be a career. It's kind of just a service project while I'm between jobs."

"Aha!" Stewart exclaimed. "You said the magic word: service. Remember, I told you that one of the keys to finding your passion and purpose is to pay close attention to the things you would do even if you didn't get paid. If you find and do those things, I can guarantee two things: First, that you will have far more impact on the world and create far more value for others than you could by doing anything else. And, second, you'll be able to figure out a way to get paid to do them so that it's economically sustainable. You'll find a niche where people value what you do so much, they'll pay you more money than you ever thought would be possible when you're having so much fun.

"I'm confident that we've found a critical clue," Stewart continued. "Now you need to learn the Third Law of Conscious Creation. You need to get your head straight so you can successfully navigate obstacles and not get derailed by them. And that's what the next law helps you do.

"As I said before, these obstacles will inevitably arise, just as you've experienced. Most people don't make it far along the journey because of this resistance. The problem is the fact that they experience events and circumstances as resistance in the first place. They label events, people, and circumstances in their life as *bad* or *good,* according to their perceptions. The truth is that they're resisting reality.

"And that's precisely the third law: *The Law of Choice and Accountability states that your perception of reality is a choice, not a condition, and your experience is your creation, whether you realize it or not. The more accountability you take for your reality, the greater power you have to change it.*

"Reality just *is,* regardless of how we perceive or label it. As Shakespeare wrote, 'There is nothing good or bad, but thinking makes it so.' And until you take ownership of your current reality, you can never change it and you can never progress. You're stuck in an illusion. You're powerless. You're chained to your negative, blame-filled perceptions. Life is hard. Your job sucks, or getting fired sucks, as the case may be. No one around you will cooperate with your idea of fairness.

"Arguing with reality leads to suffering. You told me that losing your job has been a horrible experience. But I'm confused by this because the whole reason you approached me in the first place was because you didn't like your job. The Law of Attraction worked for you. Didn't you get exactly what you wanted?"

"Well, I didn't want to be fired," Shaun protested. "I wasn't ready for that."

"What did you want, then?" Stewart asked.

"I don't know," Shaun admitted. "I guess I just wanted to ease into my purpose."

"The key words in what you just said are 'I don't know,'" Stewart said. "Furthermore, you're not even clear on your purpose either, correct?"

"Right," Shaun conceded.

"How do you expect to create your perfect world when you don't know what you want? And if you don't even know what you want, how can you be angry at any particular experience?

"The truth is that you are creating your life every moment of every day. Life isn't happening *to* you; you are responsible for your life. You are the author of your story. Now, you can author your story either unconsciously or consciously. While every human being by nature is a creator and everyone has access to the same amazing power, only some know how to create on purpose. Everyone else creates accidentally or unconsciously. Unconscious creation leads to mediocrity and misery.

"Conscious Creation, on the other hand, leads to a fulfilling life. The people who use this power on purpose create their world just the way they want it to be. And until you accept that you are responsible for everything you create, you will lack the power to create your perfect world. If you want to expand your life and means, you have to know exactly what you want, and that must be your overpowering focus.

"I must explain a nuance here: Despite our ability to choose, imagine, and create, one of the critical aspects of accepting reality is to be clear on our gifts and to realize our personal limitations. There is a pervasive belief that you can do and become anything you want to be, if you're just willing to make the effort. That is simply not true, and this type of belief can be as misleading as limiting beliefs that hold your potential hostage.

"Michael Jordan was born with specific physical capabilities, which made him a great basketball player. No matter how much I believed, and no matter how much effort I put into it, I just wasn't born to be a professional basketball player. Your True Purpose is defined as much by your gifts as by your limitations. In this sense, understanding your limitations is actually liberating, rather than constricting. It keeps you from doing things you don't enjoy, that aren't a full expression of your unique gifts and True Purpose.

"As author Parker Palmer explains, 'Each of us arrives here with a nature, which means both limits and potentials. We can learn as much about our nature by running into our limits as by experiencing our potentials. If we are to live our lives fully and well, we must learn to embrace the opposites, to live in a creative tension between our limits and our potentials. We must honor our limitations in ways that do not distort our nature, and we must trust and use our gifts in ways that fulfill the potentials God gave us.'

"So the bottom line of this law," Stewart continued, "is this: To the Conscious Creator there is reality, there is life as it is. Not how the individual sees it or how he or she thinks it should be. The Conscious Creator doesn't argue with reality, but rather takes accountability for his or her reality. Unconscious creators have a false perception of reality and are unwilling to accept reality for what it is.

"Now wait a second," Shaun interjected. "This is mostly making sense to me. But if everyone is a creator and everyone has the power to choose, then what about when other people use their power to choose in ways that hurt me? For example, I know someone who was hit by a drunk driver and is now paralyzed for the rest of his life. Would you say he created that life for himself?"

"Excellent question," Stewart said, "and that's where choice comes in. Did your friend choose to be paralyzed? Is living in a wheelchair for the rest of his life a product of his personal creation? No. But it is his unchangeable, irrefutable reality. He can argue against that reality and refuse to accept it. But no amount of protest, anger, or depression will change the reality. And if he were to wallow in anger for the rest of his life, his anger *would be* his creation. A Conscious Creator focuses on his own choices and actions, understanding that he has no control over those of others. He takes accountability for his choices and accepts his results.

"Is being paralyzed a tragedy? It certainly requires adjustments to one's life, but labeling it a tragedy is a *perception*, not an objective reality. Have you ever heard of Viktor Frankl?"

"Sure," Shaun said. "But I don't know a lot about him. Didn't he spend time in a concentration camp?"

"Yes, three years in the most inhumane, unimaginable circumstances," Stewart said. "He was a Jewish psychiatrist, and after his experience in Nazi concentration camps he published *Man's Search for Meaning*, which is one of the most important books you could ever read. In it he describes his experience and asks, 'Do the prisoners' reactions to the singular world of the concentration camp prove that man cannot escape the influences of his surroundings? Does man have no choice of action in the face of such circumstances?' He then answers his own questions."

As Stewart quoted Frankl from memory, Shaun could tell how meaningful the words were to him:

We can answer these questions from experience as well as on principle. The experiences of camp life show that man does have a choice of action. There were enough examples, often of a heroic nature, which proved that apathy could be overcome, irritability suppressed. Man can preserve a vestige of spiritual freedom, of independence of mind, even in such terrible conditions of psychic and physical stress.

We who lived in the concentration camps can remember the men who walked through the huts comforting others, giving away their last piece of bread. They may have been few in number, but they offer sufficient proof that everything can be taken away from a man but one thing: the last of the human freedoms—to choose one's attitude in any given set of circumstances, to choose one's own way.

Stewart was clearly emotional as he finished the quote, and he paused to compose himself. "That book saved me after my first business failed. I was devastated. I thought it was the end of the world. I owed so many people so much money. I was afraid they'd never speak to me again. I thought I'd never recover. But a dear friend shared Frankl's book with me, and I've never been the same since.

"Most of our beliefs are merely interpretations or subjective perceptions. And we have the undeniable power to choose to interpret events and circumstances with empowerment rather than victimhood. Victimhood is a choice, not a condition. Victimhood limits your Conscious Creation and gives your power away. If you've been wronged by another person—no matter how severe the offense—and if you hold tightly to the hurt and offense, you've ironically given your power to that individual. Refusing to forgive and seeking revenge make you a puppet on the other person's strings.

"Like victimhood, fear is also a choice, not an inevitable condition. In fact, fear doesn't even exist except as a perception that we choose. It's an illusion that we've made real. Yes, fear comes naturally to human beings. But that doesn't mean we have to be enslaved by it. Security is also largely a perception. Does a good job and a million dollars in retirement accounts make you *truly* secure, despite the *feeling* of security? Well, you've already experienced how secure a job is. And millions of Americans in recent years have discovered just how secure retirement funds are.

"Failure is also a perception that leads most people astray. They take risks without knowledge, and then they learn the wrong lessons when they fail. For example, I know a man who partnered with an unethical guy. His partner walked away with thousands of dollars and left my friend deep in debt. Sadly, the lesson my friend has taken from this is that partnerships are bad. The truth is that he made several critical mistakes along the way, yet he can't learn those lessons because he has refused to take responsibility.

"We make decisions based on our perceptions. And if our perceptions are flawed and disempowering, how can we ever make wise decisions that lead to true success, wealth, and security? And how can we ever refine our perceptions if we never analyze them consciously?

"There is a space between stimulus and response. We don't have to be captive to automated responses. Unconscious people waste their lives whining that their failures are not their fault. They'd rather absolve themselves of guilt and live a life of mediocrity than take responsibility and live a life of greatness. But to be a Conscious Creator means to live and choose from that space between stimulus and response, between events and reaction. Note that the words 'creator' and 'reactor' contain the same letters. The choice between those two options determines your destiny.

"Shaun, you've been fired. Nothing can change that reality. Now you have a choice to make. The only thing you have power over is how you choose to respond to this reality. Will you accept reality or keep arguing against it? Is this a horrible misfortune or a brilliant opportunity? Will this ruin you or propel you to future greatness?

"Napoleon Hill wrote that 'every adversity, every failure, every heartache carries with it the seed of an equal or greater benefit.' So you can focus on the immediate failure or on the seed of long-term benefit. You can use the Law of Attraction to see the positive in this event and attract greater positivity, or you can see the negative and let it drag you down even further. As a creator, you will realize that the power is yours.

"If you are the creator of how you perceive this event and how you choose to respond, then why not choose an empowering, inspiring path? What do you have to lose, other than your excuses? Why allow yourself to unconsciously submit to a life of whining and complaining? Why be a puppet on the strings of unconscious reaction? You were born for better than that, and I know you have it in you. I know you'll make the right choice. I know you're going to make it through this because of your commitment to finding your path."

Shaun was overwhelmed by the depth and amount of information Stewart had just unloaded on him. But he felt profound stirrings within himself, just as he had the first time he heard Stewart speak. And he was touched by Stewart's sincere expression of confidence in him.

"Thank you," Shaun said. "I do want to become a Conscious Creator. But I'm not sure I share your certainty in my abilities. Even though I think I get everything you're saying *in my head,* I still feel the disappointment and loss *in my heart.*"

"Listen," Stewart said, "it's not going to happen overnight. This is a process. Your subconscious mind is powerful. So is your conscious mind, but it takes vigilant consistency to train it. The false and limiting beliefs in your subconscious will constantly try to hijack your progress. But as long as you're consciously aware of that and committed to overcoming it, you will prevail.

"Now I want to go back to this clue that keeps popping up with you. It's obvious that you love to cook. I saw it in your eyes and actions when you visited Melanie and me. And now it's revealed itself with your elderly neighbor. Why do you keep resisting it? Why do you not recognize it as at least part of your bliss? And from what I've seen of you, I'd have to say it's a pretty big part of your bliss, if not the whole deal."

"I don't know," Shaun said. "I do know that I feel sparks of passion when I'm cooking. But I've always stifled it, mostly because I felt like becoming a CPA would give me greater security. Plus, it always just seemed more like a hobby. I mean, I know I could have gone to culinary school and become a chef, but I never considered it seriously because I didn't think it would be stable enough or pay well enough.

"Also, I've told you about my dad—how he is passionate but never really sticks to anything. When I was younger, I always appreciated his passion. But my mother always said, 'Passion doesn't pay the bills.' She was always the practical and grounded one in their relationship.

"As I got older, I started seeing life more from her perspective and I learned to value security over passion. So anytime I've felt passion, I've pushed it aside. In fact, my experience has taught me to be downright suspicious of passion. When I hear you speak, I feel it strongly, and I want to follow those feelings. But I feel so afraid that I'll become like my father, chasing fantastic dreams that never come true and, in the end, regretting that I didn't just stick with something I could depend on financially.

"Plus, I wouldn't really even know where to start. Like I said, I suppose I could go to culinary school, but I've already spent six years in school, and it's discouraging to think that I'd be starting over. And I could start my own business, but my lack of knowledge scares me. I'm afraid I'd fail."

"Yes, those are all understandable reasons to resist this path," Stewart said, "and I can relate to them all. They also provide perfect opportunities for you to exercise the third law. They demonstrate the inescapable truth that our beliefs determine our behavior.

"You've detailed a few assumptions, which have become ingrained into your subconscious as guiding beliefs. For example, take the belief that passion doesn't pay the bills. That passion leads to insecurity. That if you follow your passion, you'll end up like your father. Even the belief that your father has taken the wrong paths is just that—a *belief*, not a *truth*. And underlying all these beliefs are your perceptions of fear and failure.

"I invite you to investigate these assumptions and beliefs. Ask yourself whether they're objective truths or simply subjective perceptions. Furthermore, ask yourself how you're defining 'failure.' For example, suppose you were to open a restaurant, and a year later you had to close your doors because you didn't generate enough revenue or because of a legal issue. Would that be a failure?"

Shaun smiled. "Well, I know what your answer would be, but that would be a pretty big failure in my book. I suppose I could recover, but the possibility of enduring that much pain just isn't all that compelling, frankly."

"Of course," Stewart agreed. "But would you rather live from the fear of pain or from the joy of creation? Because as long as perceived pain, fear, and failure dominate your thinking and decisions, you'll never become a Conscious Creator. You'll never overcome your obstacles. When you experience them, you'll be so scarred that you won't pick yourself up and try again.

"To overcome these false and limiting beliefs, your vision of possibility and creation must be more clear and compelling than your fear. You continue to feel the fear because it's all you've been focusing on.

"So here's your next exercise: I want you to spend the next week on another exercise. I call it the Vision Plan. I want you to write your vision of your ideal life and self, in vivid detail. I also want you to stop resisting your passion for cooking. We both know that needs to be included in your vision. If you were living your ideal life, what would it look and feel like? What would you be doing as a career? How would you spend your time? How would you spend your money? Who would you be serving? Where would you live? What would your family be like? Who would your friends be? What kind of person would you be?

"I want you to be able to see, feel, smell, hear, and taste your ideal life. I want you to get so clear on it that the passion you feel when you read and envision it is stronger than the fear you feel about the possibility of perceived failure. And I think a perfect place for you to start is by writing down everything you love about cooking for your neighbor, and why. Also, think back through your life, and identify every situation and activity you've ever engaged in where you felt truly blissful. Think back on what sparked your interest and passion, where you lost track of time. Look for the common themes in all of these moments.

"All creation begins as a thought, and nothing can ever be physically created until it's first experienced as a mental creation. If you want to become a Conscious Creator, your starting point is to consciously create something in your mind. You will never progress until you envision a better future. In fact, without that vision, you can't even get started. Like most people, you'll continue to be just a slave to unconscious reaction.

"See, nature abhors a vacuum. If you don't consciously create your life—if you don't create space for possibility—then the universe will simply take you where your unconscious, unexamined beliefs steer you. As the common saying goes, *If you don't know where you're going, any road will get you there.* Or simply put, you can't get what you want until you know what you want. Without a North Star, you'll be blown wherever the wind and tides take you. Do you understand?"

"Absolutely," Shaun said. As usual, he found that Stewart could be quite convincing. "I'll get started right away." He was excited about completing the exercise.

"Excellent," Stewart said. "I look forward to seeing what you come up with."

* * *

Readers: To create your vision of your ideal life, get the Vision Plan exercise by downloading or ordering *The Conscious Creator's Reparadigming Journal* at www.ConsciousCreatorBook.com.

So far, Stewart has taught Shaun three of the Six Laws of Conscious Creation. They are:

The First Law of Conscious Creation: The Law of Attraction

You attract into your life whatever you think about the most. Your dominant and persistent thoughts eventually manifest as physical reality.

The Second Law of Conscious Creation: The Law of Purpose

For you to achieve your highest potential, your desires and actions must be manifestations of your True Self and True Purpose. Your True Self embodies the highest, most accurate truth from which you can create at your greatest potential. Conscious Creators know who they are and what they were born to accomplish.

The Third Law of Conscious Creation: The Law of Choice and Accountability

Your perception of reality is a choice, not a condition, and your experience is your creation, whether you realize it or not. The more accountability you take for your reality, the greater power you have to change it.

NINE

Amanda Wallace, professional photographer and ex-girlfriend of Shaun Porter, was in her home office, editing photographs from her last session, when the doorbell rang. It was a deliveryman with an elaborate flower bouquet. Smiling and giddy, she thanked him and closed the door. Then she smelled the flowers, opened the card, and read:

My dearest Amanda,

I would be honored if you would join me for dinner and salsa dancing this evening, wearing your red dress (you know the one). I will pick you up at 7:00. Olé!

Jim

That's just like him, she thought happily. *So romantic and spontaneous.* She hadn't even known that Jim enjoyed dancing, but he was full of surprises. Actually, when she stopped to think about it, something about the invitation made her uneasy. Still, it promised to be a wonderful evening.

It had been three months since Amanda had broken up with Shaun. She had met Jim, an artist, a month after the breakup. He was everything Shaun wasn't: spontaneous, passionate, adventurous, willing to try anything and everything with an almost reckless abandon that set her head and heart spinning. A week after their first date, he had showed her a picture he'd painted of her. It swept her off her feet—especially considering her vulnerable state.

Seven o'clock found Amanda waiting anxiously in the living room. When Jim hadn't shown up ten minutes later, she turned on the TV to distract her mind. He arrived twenty minutes later, looking sharp in a suit.

"Seven o'clock sharp, huh?" she teased.

"Forgive me, my dear," Jim implored with a slight bow. "I was so engrossed in my new painting, I lost all track of time."

"Yeah, I can tell," she said, wiping a smudge of paint off his cheek. "And you couldn't text me that you were on the way?" She was smiling as she asked, but she had to admit that his absentmindedness bothered her.

"Ah, well, you know how I am about technology," he said.

"Yeah, yeah," she said, laughing, "the bane of modern society and all."

"Exactly," he grinned, extending his arm to escort her to his scooter. He helped her put on his spare helmet. She silently bemoaned the damage it would do to her hair, but she really did enjoy riding with him.

Jim surprised her when they parked at Quiessence, one of the most lavish restaurants in the city. His artist's income wasn't exactly steady or substantial. She'd gotten used to paying for their activities.

"Surprised?" he said, noting her face. "Well, it just so happens that I sold three paintings yesterday to the premier art gallery in Phoenix. And, generous soul that I am, I've decided to share my good fortune with you."

They enjoyed a magnificent meal in magical surroundings, although

Amanda couldn't help but think that she liked Shaun's cooking even better. Jim was charming and witty as usual, and he was unusually attentive—so much so, in fact, that it increased her nervousness. Something was different. They finished their dessert, an apricot mango crème brûlée that made her swoon.

They hopped back onto the scooter and rode to a dance club—the same club where she and Shaun had taken Latin dance lessons together. Of course, she practically had to beg Shaun to take those lessons with her, but after two months they had actually made an enviable couple on the dance floor, and Shaun had surprised her with his skill and enthusiasm. As Amanda and Jim entered the club now, she fought back a flood of memories. She had been trying so hard to forget Shaun, yet in moments like this, she found it impossible.

Thankfully, after one dance with Jim, she buried the memories and was genuinely joyful. Jim was a magnificent dancer, and together they glided across the floor effortlessly. Thirty minutes later, she was breathless and glowing.

"I need a break," Jim said unexpectedly. "Come sit with me." They retired to a corner booth. Amanda was nervous, since she'd never known Jim to tire so quickly. She was surprised to note that he suddenly looked nervous as well.

"Listen," he said, obviously struggling for words. This was definitely a first for him, she noted. "I'm sorry. I had this all planned out, but now that I'm here, I can't remember a thing."

Amanda sat still. The nervousness she'd been feeling all day sat cold in the pit of her stomach.

He continued, rushing his speech now, "I've never known anyone who makes me feel like you do. I've never had so much fun with anyone. Ever since I met you, I've felt more inspired than I ever have. I stay up late every night painting, because I get so many ideas when I'm with you. The truth is that I'm madly, deeply in love with you. I know we haven't been dating long. I know I'm not the most dependable guy. And maybe I'm crazy, but I feel so sane and alive when I'm with you."

Jim knelt then and took her hand. "Amanda, I want you to be my wife. I want to make you happy. Will you marry me?"

Amanda was stunned. She had known they were somewhat serious, but she never would have guessed he'd be this serious, this soon. Yes, she had been infatuated with him, but this proposal bowled her over. With startling clarity, all she could think of was the fantasies she had envisioned of this moment with Shaun—the moment that had never come. The absence of it had broken her heart.

Her dramatic pause had revealed too much.

"Listen," Jim said with a note of desperation, "I know this is sudden. But it just feels so right. I know we can be happy together. Just give me a chance."

"I'm so sorry," she said, collecting her thoughts. "You are an amazing man. I love being with you. But I'm just not ready." Fighting tears, she excused herself to the bathroom, locked herself in a stall, and cried for several minutes. When she emerged, eyes red and makeup smudged, she found him waiting in the lobby. They rode home in silence.

Jim walked Amanda to the door and made one last-ditch effort. "Will you just promise me to think about it?" he implored.

"I'm sorry, Jim, but my answer is no," she said, and then retreated inside. She spent a sleepless, emotionally draining night, deep in thought. In the morning, she called her father, the person she always trusted to help her make difficult decisions.

"Hi, honey!" he greeted her cheerfully.

"Daddy," she started. Then she broke down.

"Are you okay?" he asked, the concern evident in his voice.

"I'm sorry," she said. "I'm okay. I just need to talk. Do you have time today?"

"For you? Anytime. Tell me when and where."

"As soon as possible. I'm sorry. I don't want to be a burden, but I really need you."

"Tell you what," he said. "I'll cancel my first appointment of the morning and be right over."

Amanda's father arrived thirty minutes later. They hugged, he kissed her on the forehead, and they sat on the couch. "What's going on, baby?" he asked.

"Jim asked me to marry him last night," she blurted. "I turned him down. And I'm so confused about why. Jim is everything I told Shaun I wanted him to be. He's fun and passionate. He's not afraid to take risks. I love being with him. He makes me laugh. He treats me with respect. I told Shaun I was ready for marriage, and now that I've found the perfect guy, I've got cold feet. What's wrong with me?"

Her father must have known that she just needed to talk, because he simply waited for her to go on.

"When he asked me," she continued, "all I could think of was Shaun. But that's silly because it's *so* over with him. And as much as Jim excites me, he worries me, too. Shaun was dependable and responsible. He was a rock in my life, just like you. In fact, he always reminded me of you. Steady, you know? I just always knew he'd be there for me. Well, except for when I needed him most," she added bitterly.

"And Jim, well, he's fun and exciting, but sometimes I just don't know where he is. He's so unpredictable. I like how adventurous he is, but sometimes it seems like he's so crazy, he doesn't even have his head screwed on right—like he's oblivious to consequences. I enjoy moments and days with him, but I just have a hard time seeing him in my long-term future. I've always worried that he was just a rebound relationship for me. And sometimes I get the feeling that his passion is just on the surface, nothing that really comes from deep inside."

"All sizzle and no steak?" her father offered.

"Exactly!" she exclaimed. "With Shaun, I always felt that if he were to just let go of his fears and find his passion, he'd really commit to something no matter what it took. But I've always worried that Jim would be too flighty to stick with anything. Shaun is too fearful, and Jim is too reckless."

"Doesn't sound to me like there's anything wrong with *you*," her father said. "I know what you're going through is tough, but it sounds to me like you've got it pretty well figured out."

"Then why does it hurt so much?" asked Amanda.

"Because you know exactly what you want and you know you can't get it from either of them," her father answered.

"Do you think I want too much? Am I just being too picky? Should I learn to accept what worries me about either of them and just deal with it?"

"Well, you're asking the wrong person," he replied with a grin, "because no guy on the planet is good enough for my baby." He answered seriously then: "No, I don't think you're wanting too much. You know, I've always told you that who you marry is the most important decision you'll ever make. My advice to you would be to take a break from guys for a while. Pamper yourself. Do something exciting *just for you*. That's the best thing I can say: Just take your time. You're twenty-eight years old, and I know you're ready for a family, but don't rush this. You know what you want, and that's ninety percent of the battle to get it.

"Darling, you're too good to settle. You can't control or change Shaun, Jim, or anyone else. All you can do is be the best person you can be. Be the person your dream guy would want to marry. When you do that and you're patient, I guarantee you'll find him, and he'll be ready for you."

Teary-eyed, she said, "Thanks, Daddy. You always know just what to say."

"Well, I don't know about that," he said modestly. "I think it's more that you're just a great decision maker." He choked up then. "I just wish your mother could have been here for you. I'm sure she would have been much better at this than me. I know how proud she would be of you. And you know what she would tell you, right?"

"Of course," Amanda answered, as she burst into tears again. He held her tightly as she sobbed, thinking of her mother's last words to her as she lay dying of cancer, when Amanda was seventeen. *Live your life to have no regrets,* her mother had whispered the last time Amanda had ever seen her.

Several minutes passed as father and daughter held each other.

Finally composed, Amanda said, "I'm sorry you canceled your appointment for this."

"Not at all," he assured her. "You know I'm here for you anytime you need me."

"I know," she said. "Thank you so much."

After her father left, Amanda went back to bed and slept soundly for hours. She awoke in the late afternoon, feeling comforted and refreshed. She had dreamed of walking through a majestic cathedral, and it reminded her of Shaun telling her about his European trip with his father. She had fallen in love with him then, seeing the glow in his eyes, feeling the passion in his voice.

Realizing she hadn't eaten since dinner the night before at Quiessence, she went to the kitchen to fix a late lunch. There, on the refrigerator, she saw the plaque with bold letters. Her life's motto, as she'd learned from her mother: *No regrets.*

Suddenly, she knew exactly what she was going to do. Without hesitation, she went to her computer, canceled all her photography sessions, and booked a one-way flight to London.

TEN

Two days after his conversation with Stewart, Shaun hadn't begun his Vision Plan exercise. He wanted to take his time with it, really go deep and do it right. At least, that's what he told himself. The real problem was that he was scared—scared to go inside himself, scared of what he might discover, scared of getting it wrong. He was plagued by an inner resistance he'd never felt before. So he procrastinated.

A week passed. Shaun continued cooking for Dorothy. He rode his mountain bike. He went hiking. He pondered. He also watched his savings account balance drop, which made him worry.

Another week passed. One day Shaun arrived home from food shopping and discovered an e-mail from an accounting firm in Seattle.

Mr. Porter,

Your previous boss, Ryan Newton, referred us to you. When we explained what we're looking for, he immediately told us about you and said you had shared with him some outside-the-box ideas. He said you weren't the best fit for Alliance, but he recommended you highly for us.

As an innovative accounting and business consulting firm, we're looking for innovators like you. We're confident you'll appreciate our entrepreneurial and flexible culture. We offer much more than tax preparation for our clients, including strategic business advice based on accounting data.

We're prepared to offer qualified candidates an extremely competitive salary, along with a signing bonus and one of the best benefits packages in the industry. And, of course, chosen candidates will have their relocation costs reimbursed.

I invite you to meet with us in person, any day of your choosing in the next two weeks. Please let us know which day works for you, and we will make travel arrangements, all on our dime.

I look forward to meeting you.

Sincerely,
Brad Wilcox
Wilcox & Partners, CPAs & Strategic Business Consultants

Shaun felt simultaneously thrilled and alarmed. Was this an opportunity for him to apply his ideas and gain new experience, or was it simply a distraction from his True Purpose? He was tempted to immediately say yes, but he decided to sleep on it. The next morning he decided to at least go for an interview. What could it hurt? If nothing else, he could use a mini-retreat. He responded, and the date was set.

The following week, as Shaun's plane descended toward the Seattle airport, he gazed down and found the rich green earth a refreshing change from the Arizona desert. He felt like a VIP when he was greeted by a driver, who took him to a plush hotel. He enjoyed a good meal and then relaxed in the hot tub and pool.

The next morning Shaun was picked up by the same driver and taken to the Wilcox & Partners office, where he was first given a tour. Though not large, the office was impressive. The modern architecture and elegant interior decorating made him feel important, like this was a place for serious producers. Inspirational posters, unlike anything in the drab CPA offices he was used to, adorned the walls. This was clearly an environment not for compliant number crunchers but for innovative movers and shakers.

Shaun had been expecting to interview with a midlevel manager, but instead he was ushered into Brad Wilcox's office. Brad asked him to share the presentation he had shown to his ex-boss, Ryan. Brad listened intently, offering ideas and insights throughout. The energy was high, and Shaun felt an instant connection with Brad. It was obvious they could work well together.

Brad shared details about a few clients the firm was working with and asked for Shaun's ideas. Based on his previous brainstorming, which hadn't been appreciated at Alliance, Shaun was bursting with ideas. Two hours later, they were interrupted by Brad's secretary on the speakerphone, telling Brad it was time for his next appointment. Brad told her he was almost done, and then he sat thinking for a moment.

"Shaun," he said, "I'm *very* impressed with you. Your ideas are just what we're looking for. Dutiful number crunchers who just do what they're told don't cut it here—they don't take us where we want to go. We need strategic thinkers like you to take our firm to the next level. I've never done this on a first interview before, but I'm willing to take a risk with you. I'd like you to come and work with us. I'd like you to start as soon as possible. And I'm willing to pay you $85,000 a year to make it happen. As I mentioned in my e-mail, we'll pay for your moving costs—and we'll throw in a $10,000 signing bonus. What do you say?"

Shaun gulped and tried to remain cool. His annual salary with Alliance had been $60,000. His deep reservations, based on what he'd been learning from Stewart, were buried by glittering dollar signs. Before he could even think, he heard himself blurt, "I accept. I think I can really fit in and make a difference here."

"It's settled then," Brad said. "How soon do you think you can move?"

"Well, I really don't have anything keeping me in Phoenix," Shaun said, even as Amanda's face flashed painfully through his mind. "I could be here in a couple weeks, if that works for you."

"Excellent," Brad said. "I'll send you over to HR to work out the details."

Shaun flew home the next day in a daze. He'd never considered leaving Phoenix. He never thought he'd find an accounting firm like this. He was surprised—and worried—by his own spontaneity. Some inner misgiving nagged his subconscious. But he wasn't about to pass up that salary.

He spent the next two weeks packing, putting his home on the market, finding an apartment in Seattle online, and saying good-bye to family and friends. He spent one last evening with Dorothy. Tearfully, she hugged him and thanked him profusely for all he'd done for her. While packing, Shaun discovered his notebook. On the top page he'd written *My Vision of My Ideal Life*. Guiltily, he tucked the notebook into a box and tried to forget about it. He thought about sending an e-mail to Stewart, but decided against it.

Throughout the week, even stronger than his nagging guilt over not finishing his assignment from Stewart, one thought dominated his mind: Amanda. But with his pride still stinging from the breakup, he resisted the urge to call her. The night before he was to leave, however, he caved and called.

Butterflies fluttered in his stomach as the phone rang. He was just about to chicken out and hang up when Amanda's voicemail clicked on.

"Hey, you've reached Amanda's cell," her voice said. "I'll be out of the country for at least a month. Maybe longer. Who knows. So feel free to leave me a message, but understand that I probably won't return your call anytime soon. I'll have limited Internet access, so you can try shooting me an e-mail, but no guarantees that I'll respond. Bye for now."

That's strange, he thought. A pang of jealousy stabbed him as the thought crossed his mind that she could be traveling with another guy. They'd always talked about traveling through Europe together . . .

"Hey, it's me. Shaun," he said haltingly. "So . . . I'm calling to say good-bye. I never really did get a chance to say it before. I've taken a job in Seattle, and I'm leaving tomorrow. I have no idea when you'll get this message, but I just wanted you to know. I hope you're doing well."

He paused and weighed his next words carefully. "I miss you."

He hung up quickly, fighting tears.

Shaun awoke early the next morning, placed a picture of Amanda on the dashboard of his car, and started the long drive to Seattle.

ELEVEN

Shaun sat at his desk surreptitiously surfing the Web. He felt a little guilty, but he couldn't help himself. He was in search of specialty ingredients for a recipe he'd been perfecting, as well as researching ideas for next week's cooking class.

It had been two months since he'd moved to Seattle. He loved the city and was surprised by how readily he'd adjusted to the change in climate. He enjoyed his job. As Brad had promised, he was given a lot of flexibility and opportunities to innovate. He liked problem-solving for his clients. It was satisfying whenever their business improved because of his recommendations. He was working with several different clients in different industries and with different challenges, and he enjoyed the variety. And, of course, he relished depositing his checks and watching his savings account grow again.

He also appreciated that the hours were reasonable. So far he hadn't worked more than forty hours in a week. This allowed him to focus his evenings on honing his cooking skills and creating new recipes, especially since he didn't have much else to do—the only people he knew in town were coworkers and clients.

Stewart's observation about his cooking had unleashed a passion Shaun wasn't able to stifle. He liked his job, but he *loved* cooking. It had always been part of his life, but now that he was more conscious of his gift, it took hold of him, distracting him during the day and consuming his evenings. He would catch himself brainstorming recipes during meetings with clients.

As an outgrowth of the passion he'd discovered on his European trip when he was eighteen, Shaun was drawn deeper and deeper into fusion cuisine: combining elements of culinary styles from different countries. He experimented with a carefree abandon he'd never felt before. Sometimes his experiments resulted in dismal, hardly edible failures. But other times his wildly creative combinations would result in a dish so spectacular he felt like a famous chef. He longed to share such dishes.

He missed his evenings with Dorothy. To test his recipes, he had started looking for any opportunity to cook for people. He couldn't resist watching his "guinea pigs" take that first bite and seeing their reaction, especially with his most creative recipes. On the weekends he surprised neighbors with dinner. He occasionally brought lunch for coworkers. He even cooked for clients. In fact, one comment from a client had given him a jolt. After taking a bite of his glazed quail with grilled pineapple, the client had said, only half joking, "Shaun, are you sure you're in the right line of work? I think I'd pay you more to cook for me than to consult with me." That unforgettable comment plagued his thoughts.

When Shaun cooked for an office party, Brad's wife, Rachel, took him aside and said, "Shaun, we've had our parties catered by some of the best restaurants in town, and I swear we've never had anything this good. Did you go to cooking school before becoming an accountant?"

Shaun laughed. "Not unless you count cooking shows on TV. I've just always loved it. I can't really remember not knowing how to cook."

"Are you sure you didn't miss your calling in life?" Rachel asked.

Her innocent comment, coming in the wake of the client's similar question, cut deep. He felt he couldn't discuss his feelings about his career with his boss's wife, so he tried to brush it off. "Nah, it's just a hobby."

"Well, listen," she said, "I volunteer at a troubled-youth facility. We've talked about offering classes to help the kids learn life skills, expose them to new experiences, get them interested in something. Someone brought up cooking, but we've never been able to find someone to teach the class. Would you be interested in something like that? It would just be a volunteer position, probably one night a week. They'll pay for your supplies, but unfortunately I don't think they have the budget to pay you."

"Done," Shaun said eagerly. "Tell me when and where I start."

The details were worked out, and thus began his weekly Thursday evening cooking class for at-risk young people, mostly teenagers. He found that on Thursdays he couldn't wait to leave work and get to the class. He came alive with the teens. His passion was contagious, and the counselors began reporting that the kids were much more cooperative and happy and much less inclined to self-destructive behavior.

The counselors started attending his classes to see what he was doing that was so special. Occasionally, his students would bring their visiting parents to the class, excited to share what they were learning. Shaun got used to seeing visitors, so he hardly noticed the quiet, dark-haired man who visited frequently. The man would observe Shaun's instructions for a few minutes, help himself to a bite of whatever they were cooking, and then leave as quietly as he came.

One day at work, as Shaun searched the Internet for where to buy several exotic ingredients, Brad walked into his office.

"Hey, Shaun."

Shaun quickly closed out of his Internet browser. "Hey, Brad. What's up?"

"I've got some good news and some bad news. The bad news is, Denise just let me know that she's moving in a month."

"Really? I thought she loved it here. And isn't she extremely popular with her clients?" Shaun asked.

"Yes on both counts," Brad said ruefully. "I hate to see her go. But her husband just accepted a promotion, and they've decided it's the right thing for them."

"So what's the good news?" Shaun asked.

"I'd like you to take her clients," Brad said. "I've really appreciated your work. You may not be as experienced as Denise, but you make up for it with your fresh thinking and innovative ideas. You've got some big shoes to fill, but I think you're the one. You up for the challenge? And if it helps your decision, it'll mean a $6,000 a year raise for you."

"So does this mean I'll be giving up some of my clients?" Shaun asked.

"Actually, no," Brad said. "It will mean longer hours for you, at least until we can find someone else. Is that a problem?"

Shaun thought for a moment. His only worry was that it would cut into his evening cooking sessions. But, as before, he found the money compelling. And the promotion stroked his ego. Denise had some high-profile clients, and the fact that Brad trusted Shaun with them said a lot.

"No problem. I'm in," Shaun said.

"Great. I'll have you start working with Denise before she leaves so you can make a smooth transfer."

With that, Shaun's forty-hour workweek became a sixty-hour workweek. With the help of Brad's wife, he was able to preserve his Thursday evenings for cooking class. But his frustration mounted as each evening he seemed to get home later and later, leaving less and less time for experimentation in the kitchen. Weekends became highly treasured, as they were the only time he could go deep enough into his passion to create new recipes.

And throughout it all he wondered what he was ever going to tell Stewart, and when. So he was both pleased and flustered when, a month into his frantic schedule, he received an e-mail from Stewart.

Shaun,

I'm just checking in to see how you're doing with the laws and to see if you've written your vision of your ideal life. I haven't heard from you in a while. I hope everything is going well.

Stewart

His conscience nagging him, Shaun ignored the e-mail for a couple of days. He finally mustered the courage to respond.

Stewart,

Thanks for checking in. I have to be honest with you: I haven't completed the assignment. And I did something big that I suspect you won't approve of. Several months ago I was offered a great accounting and consulting job in Seattle. I couldn't resist the salary, so I took the job.

I don't know if it's my True Purpose, but it is fulfilling and I'm enjoying myself. (Although I have to admit that the long hours are wearing on me. Also, the weekly cooking class with troubled teens that I volunteer for is actually much more satisfying than my job.)

And isn't there something to be said for all the money I'm saving? I'm putting away $2,500 a month. Couldn't that be a wise way to go—to focus on money at least for a short time in order to save for one's True Purpose?

Shaun

He nervously clicked SEND, almost certain of how Stewart would respond. Sure enough, the response came the next day.

Shaun,

The problem isn't that you took the job, but rather why you took the job. It was clearly a reactive decision. You have no North Star, so you're drifting wherever the winds and waves of circumstances take you. Just because this took you in a seemingly positive direction doesn't negate the fact that you're drifting, rather than navigating toward a fixed, immovable point. You have no defined framework for making decisions—other than the predictable (and deceiving) goals of money and security.

You know what my answer is to your money question. You can spend your entire life chasing money, only to discover in the end that it's just not worth it. Making money is easy. The real challenge is to pursue purpose no matter what. And that results in a far more fulfilling—and profitable—life than chasing money.

Shaun, think about this deeply: Who are you? To what end were you created? You must know this if you are to create the world you want and fulfill the measure of your creation.

I can't force you to define your North Star and pursue your True Purpose. But we had a deal that I'd mentor you as long as you did the work. Since you're not doing the work, we can't continue with the remaining Laws of Conscious Creation. And without all six laws, powerful creation is not possible.

I leave you with these questions: Is any amount of money worth leaving your true gifts undeveloped, your True Purpose unfulfilled? Do you want to be an actor in someone else's script, or do you want to write your own?

Regretfully,
Stewart

TWELVE

Aaron Weiss checked his bank account to make sure the funds had been transferred. He stared at the number, deep in thought. He thought of calling his mother, but his modesty prevailed. His parents had had high hopes for him when they'd sent him to America for college, but he knew they had never dreamed this big.

He closed his computer screen and went downstairs, where he found his wife, Ilana, reading. He bent down to kiss her cheek.

"So it's done, then?" Ilana asked.

"Yes," he said, joining her on the sofa. "One more chapter closed."

At forty-six years old, Aaron had just sold his third business, a language software company that had been struggling when he bought it six years earlier. When he researched it, he had immediately seen the potential and known exactly how to grow it.

"You sound almost sad about it. I thought you were ready to move on. What, that isn't enough money for you?" his wife teased.

Aaron smiled. "No, it's not that. I'm just thinking about what to do with the money. It's not ours, you know."

"I'm sure you'll think of something world-changing," she said. "You always have."

"Well, for one," he said, "I'd like to donate more to the youth home, at least enough for them to start paying some of their volunteers. We've got a few whom I'd really like to keep for good."

"You should talk to Brad," she said. "He may have a few ideas."

"Yes, I had the same thought," he concurred. "But the first thing I'm going to do is take my beautiful wife to the finest restaurant in town. I already have reservations for tonight."

"As if you need an excuse for that," she said. "You ought to just buy the restaurant and make it official."

"Now there's a thought," he said. Aaron and Rachel were frugal about most things, but fine dining was the one of the few areas where they didn't mind spending a lot of money. "What I'm really looking for," Aaron continued, "is some unique way to bridge cultures. We have a chance to do something big now."

"Still not over Khalid?" Ilana asked gently.

"You know I never have been," he said with pain in his voice. "There was just no need for that, and I'll do anything to stop it from happening to other boys."

"You can't fix the world, you know," she said. "Those problems are much deeper than your pocketbook. Even now."

"I know, I know," he said. "But that doesn't mean that I can't try, that I can't do my part."

She hugged him tenderly. "You've already done plenty, Aaron. You're a good man."

He kissed her head. "Maybe. But there's still so much to do."

THIRTEEN

It was one o'clock in the morning, and Shaun was feverishly flinging gourmet ingredients about, then synthesizing them like a chemist. Sweating, he bounced madly from stove top to bowl to counter, tending to every aspect of the intricate recipe. He had lost track of time.

Despite the fact that work still dominated his life, Shaun's fusion cuisine experiments had become an irresistible pull on his remaining time. He'd stayed up cooking until at least three a.m. each night for the past three weeks. He dreamed of cooking and woke up each morning with new ideas for fantastic combinations. For the past five days and nights, Shaun had been obsessed with a particular recipe: grilled spiced lamb chops with cilantro vinaigrette and an exotic potato salad. He had envisioned and even tasted it in a dream. He had never before had such piercing clarity about anything in his life. He knew precisely how it should look and taste. After several experiments, he had finally perfected the seasoning on the lamb chops and potato salad. But no matter how desperately Shaun tried, he couldn't get the vinaigrette to complement the lamb just right.

Finally, the previous morning, he had awoken knowing the precise ingredient he needed. He went to work but struggled to concentrate. He rushed to a specialty store during his lunch break to grab the precious ingredient. He had tried to leave work by nine that night, but a hard deadline had forced him to stay an agonizing two more hours. He had finally arrived home at eleven thirty and hadn't even taken time to change his clothes.

By two a.m. Shaun had finished. As he dished the meal onto a plate, he realized he was breathing hard, as if he'd been exercising. He sat at his table and just stared at the plate for several moments, almost too anxious to take a bite. Finally, he cut a small portion of lamb chop, dipped it into the vinaigrette, and slowly raised it to his mouth. He chewed meticulously, his senses heightened to their peak. His eyes closed, he moaned. His shoulders relaxed, and he melted into his seat.

It was *very* close, the best effort so far. But it was still missing something. Then it hit him. "Of course!" he jumped out of his seat. "Why didn't I think of that before?"

Shaun rummaged frantically through his cupboards. He thought he had the ingredient left over from a previous recipe, but it was nowhere to be found. And the only store he knew of that sold it was clear across town.

He swore out loud. There was no way he was going to wait until after work. Almost without thinking, he called the office, dialed Brad's extension, and left a voicemail.

"Brad, this is Shaun. I'm sorry, but I'm not feeling well. Can you have someone cover for me today? Thanks."

He hung up, feeling guilty. He'd never lied to an employer before. Stifling the guilt, he cleaned the kitchen and then enjoyed a long, hot shower. He tried to sleep, but tossed and turned until five a.m. At seven thirty he bounded out of bed and quickly dressed, not even noticing the blinking light on his answering machine. He drove an hour to the specialty store.

By nine a.m. he was in the kitchen again, a mad scientist on the verge of a major breakthrough. By eleven thirty the dish was ready. Quivering with anxiety and excitement, Shaun wiped the sweat off his forehead and neck, and once again he sat down to take the first bite. This time, he was almost too afraid to go through with it; he didn't think he could recover if this one didn't work out. But he forced himself to take a bite.

Time stood still. Feeling like Michelangelo must have felt removing the scaffolding and gazing at the completed Sistine Chapel ceiling for the first time, Shaun closed his eyes and chewed.

The rapturous flavor of perfection staggered him. "Oooh, yes," he moaned deeply. He jumped out of his chair and pumped his fist into the air. "*Yes!*" he yelled. "Yes, yes, yes, yes, yes!" He raised both arms to the heavens and shouted, "I'm a genius!"

He sank back into his chair. He had never felt quite this emotional in his life, and he almost wondered if something was wrong with him. But nothing had ever felt so right before.

He composed himself and then finished the most amazing meal of his life, taking his time and moaning in sheer pleasure with every bite. As he took the last bite, an idea leaped into his head for a chicken recipe that would also go perfectly with the vinaigrette. A plan for combining the spices flowed through him as if he were plugged into a divine outlet.

Shaun jumped up to grab a pen and paper so he could get the recipe down before he lost it. As he finished writing it, he noticed his blinking voicemail button. It slowly dawned on him that he'd skipped work without even knowing if Brad had approved the "sick" day. He pushed the button.

"Shaun, this is Brad," came the voice. "I got your message. I hope you're doing all right. Hey, I'm sure you need some rest, but we've got some reports building up. Do the best you can, but we'd really appreciate some help if you could make it even for just a couple hours today."

Shaun groaned. After his almost spiritual experience, he couldn't bear the thought of going in to work. And that's when it struck him like a two-by-four across the face.

What the hell am I doing with my life?

He collapsed onto his couch, his head in his hands, staring into space, overwhelmed by the awful realization that he had accepted the wrong job for the wrong reasons. *Why am I not living my passion?* he thought. *What if I could do this every day of my life?*

In that moment, everything Stewart had taught him finally sank in and clicked. Shaun finally accepted that everything in his life until that point had been a fear-based rejection of his purpose for existing. *All those wasted years. What's wrong with me?*

As he pondered his life decisions, a deep panic arose within him. Suddenly, he knew exactly what he needed to do. He dashed to his bedroom and ransacked it in search of what he had almost intentionally misplaced, what he had wanted to forget about. But there it was: his notebook, which had remained empty since Stewart's last assignment.

He seized it and began writing his vision of his ideal life. The words poured from his soul. The stream of consciousness was unrelenting. Ideas crawled from the nooks and crannies of his mind, impressions he'd had years ago but ignored. He became so engrossed that the vision almost felt real to him. Three hours later, he had written twenty-six pages, and the river of ideas slowed to a trickle. It dawned on him that his fingers were cramped, his back was aching, and he was hungry and exhausted.

Shaun warmed and relished another helping of his magnum opus, then crawled into bed and slept soundly for several hours. When he awoke, he went for a thirty-minute bike ride on the trails behind his apartment, then returned and reread what he had written.

After sleeping, he was able to clarify, organize, and fine-tune the grandiose and scattered vision. He condensed and focused his far-ranging thoughts into three pages of a concrete and clear vision. With that in place, his thoughts turned to how he would get from where he was to where he wanted to be.

That's where he got stuck. He knew he needed Stewart's help, though he didn't feel worthy of it. But brimming with passion and clutched by determination, a spontaneous urge he'd felt before swept over him. He called work and guiltily left another message for Brad, then called the youth home to cancel his cooking class that evening. Then he jumped online and, paying a premium to fly the next day, booked a ticket to Fresno.

FOURTEEN

Rain-soaked and bedraggled, Shaun rang Stewart's doorbell at ten thirty at night.

His flight had been delayed. The rental car company only had one car left, which had just been turned in and hadn't been refueled. They weren't going to let him take it, but they had finally relented to Shaun's pleading. Lost in thought and anxious that Stewart would reject him, Shaun had spaced out on the need to gas up. He ran out of gas two miles from Stewart's house and had walked, dragging his suitcase, the rest of the way in the rain.

Tension knotted in his stomach. The last time he'd done this it had turned out okay. But Stewart's last e-mail had changed things.

The porch light came on and Stewart opened the door, wearing a robe.

"Shaun? What are you doing here at this time of night?"

"I'm so sorry for surprising you again," Shaun said. "I'll totally understand if you want me to leave. But I'm desperate to get some questions answered. If I could just have half an hour, I'm happy to be on my way."

Stewart was visibly perturbed. "Where's your car? How did you even get here?"

Shaun explained what had happened, then pleaded, "Please forgive me. I know I don't deserve your help. But I would be so grateful if you could just give me some insights to help me get unstuck."

"I thought I made it clear in my last e-mail that we were done."

"Does it make any difference that I've completed your last assignment?" Shaun asked.

"Well, that was three months ago."

Shaun heard Melanie call from the house, "Stewart, who is it?"

"It's Shaun Porter," Stewart called back.

"Well, what are you doing? Let him in!" she commanded.

"Come on in," Stewart said reluctantly.

Shaun entered tentatively. Melanie walked down the hall and said warmly, "Shaun, it's nice to see you again. But it *is* a little late. What are you up to?"

Shaun explained again.

"And this guy wasn't even going to let you in?" Melanie said, glowering at Stewart.

"I'm sorry, Shaun, you just caught me at a bad time," Stewart said. "Tell you what. We'll put you up for the night, and in the morning we'll help you get your car gassed up. Do you have a return flight?"

"Yes, on Sunday afternoon," Shaun said.

"Listen, Shaun, I appreciate that you made the effort to come out here. You're welcome to stay until Sunday. But I've got a busy schedule tomorrow. I won't be able to take any time with you."

"I completely understand," Shaun said glumly. "I'm sorry for the surprise."

"Oh, don't let this guy get you down," Melanie encouraged. "You're welcome here anytime, and I'm sure you'll figure things out. Follow me. Let's get you into some dry clothes. Are you hungry?"

"Yes, I am," Shaun said. "I didn't stop to eat at the airport. I just wanted to get here as fast as possible. I didn't even buy my ticket until last night."

Melanie escorted him to the guest room. "Get changed and then come to the kitchen. I'll throw something together for you."

"Thank you so much," Shaun said. "I apologize for the hassle. Please forgive me."

"Maybe you can make it up to us by cooking for us while you're here," Melanie said with a grin.

"I'd love to," Shaun said.

Shaun changed his clothes and slunk to the kitchen. After forcing himself to eat the sandwich Melanie had made for him, he went to the guest room. He crumpled onto the bed, deeply discouraged and beating himself up for procrastinating on the Vision Plan assignment. He tossed and turned for several hours, finally dropping into fitful sleep at two thirty a.m.

Shaun had planned to offer to cook breakfast for his hosts. But the frantic trip, combined with the recent exhausting breakthrough, had caught up with him, and he didn't wake up until nine o'clock the next morning. He dressed and shambled to the kitchen, where he was surprised to find Stewart waiting for him.

"Shaun, I've changed my mind. Grab a bite to eat, and then join me in the library."

Shaun wolfed down his breakfast, thanked Melanie profusely, and hurried to the library.

"Shaun," Stewart began, "I apologize for being so short with you last night. I really do admire your boldness. It's just that, as I told you last night, you caught me at a bad time." He paused and looked down.

Shaun was surprised to note that Stewart was suddenly emotional.

Stewart looked back up, his eyes glistening. "You've heard me speak about my mentor, Wayne Christofferson?"

Shaun nodded.

"Yesterday was the tenth anniversary of his death. He meant so much to me. As I do every year, I visited his grave yesterday. It's always a tough day for me.

"Last night Melanie reminded me of the time I arrived on Wayne's doorstep late one night after my first business had failed. I'm sure I looked even more pathetic than you looked last night," he said, grinning.

Shaun smiled and ducked his head, embarrassed. "Yeah, I *felt* pretty pathetic."

"I know the feeling," Stewart said. "But thankfully, Wayne was incredibly patient with me. I owe all my success to him. And to honor him, I'd like to spend some time with you today. I do have my son's soccer game in an hour, but I've rearranged my afternoon schedule."

"Thank you," Shaun said. "You didn't have to do that."

"And Wayne didn't have to do anything for me," Stewart said. "Come here. I want to show you something." He stood, and Shaun followed him to a glass case at the far corner of the library. Inside the case were dozens of books.

"These are what Wayne gave to me when he died," Stewart said, looking over the books reverently. "The last time I saw him, he told me that this collection would be infinitely more valuable to me than money or anything else he could give me. I've spent years poring over these books and studying his marked passages. This is how I discovered the Six Laws of Conscious Creation.

"You'll learn, Shaun, that these laws are universal. I've put them into a form that works for me, but I'm not the first to teach them. The wisest men and women have repeated them through the ages. They're waiting for anyone to discover. But to discover them, you must love truth more than money, more than excuses, more than the fear of change. Discovering these laws takes humility to accept that you may be blinded by false and limiting beliefs.

"And that's exactly what I want to teach you today, Shaun. I want to teach you how to overcome false beliefs to gain more power in your life." He suddenly choked up.

Shaun waited, honored by Stewart's vulnerability.

Stewart sat down again, motioning Shaun to do the same. He composed himself and continued, "Wayne had always been there for me. Until he wasn't. When he died, I was angry. I took it personally, as if he had willingly left me, just as my father did. It took me a long time to process and overcome those wounds. I had developed some crippling false beliefs because of them. I was only able to recognize and replace those false beliefs by studying these books and discovering the fourth law."

Stewart leaned forward. "Shaun, one of the reasons I was hesitant to continue our discussions is because I just didn't want to see you ignore the truth as long as *I* did. The first three laws are true and vital. But it's really this fourth law that gives power to the Law of Attraction. This is where it all comes together, where you start getting power to apply the laws to achieve your vision. I wanted to make sure you were ready."

"Stewart, I can't tell you how sorry I am for taking so long with my last assignment," Shaun said. "But I have done it. I did it just two days ago, after having a major breakthrough. So now I have my vision, but I still feel stuck. I'm just not sure where to start. But I can tell you that I'm ready to do the work. Whatever you say."

"Can I see what you wrote—your vision?" Stewart asked. "Did you bring it with you?"

"I did. I'll go grab it." Shaun retrieved his notebook from his suitcase, rejoined Stewart in the library, and gave him the notes.

Stewart read in silence for several minutes, nodding periodically. He finished and looked up at Shaun. "I've done this exercise with a lot of people, but this is the clearest vision statement I've ever read," he said.

"Well, it certainly feels clear to me," Shaun said. "Although I admit it was much longer in coming than it should have been."

"So what prompted the breakthrough?" Stewart asked.

Shaun explained everything he'd gone through over the past few months. "And so when I realized how much I dreaded going into work after what I'd just been through," he said, "that did it. It was everything you've been trying to tell me. I realized that no amount of money was worth feeling that dread. I realized the feeling I felt while perfecting that recipe was worth any struggle I may have to go through."

"Ah," Stewart noted, "spoken by a man who truly gets it. And I'm glad you said the word 'struggle,' because achieving this vision *will* be a struggle. What you've outlined here is fairly ambitious, and dreams like this aren't achieved overnight."

"Yes, I do realize that," Shaun said. "And that's exactly what I hoped you could help me with. I really don't even know how to get started. I mean, a CPA doesn't just quit his job and open a revolutionary restaurant like this."

"Yes, this is going to take a few foundational steps," Stewart agreed.

"Do you have any practical ideas for me?" Shaun asked. "How can I get from where I am to where I want to go? What's my next step?"

"This goes much deeper than practicality," Stewart said. "You first need to learn more principles. Specifically, you need to know how to gather your power through alignment. You also need to understand how to be patient, to do the right things for a long enough period of time for your vision to unfold. Finally, you need to learn how to act in faith. And those are the remaining three Laws of Conscious Creation."

"Are you going to teach me all of them today?" Shaun asked eagerly.

"Actually, no. We'll start with the fourth law, which is critical. The absence of this law in particular is the greatest reason why the Law of Attraction, at face value, doesn't work for most people. I really want to take our time with this fourth law to make sure you get it. It's the one least understood and most often neglected by everyone I've ever taught. I don't want you to make that mistake."

"You're the boss," Shaun said. "I'm all ears."

"Well, let me get to my soccer game, and we'll start when I get back. Help yourself to anything in the kitchen. And of course, you're welcome to jump in the pool or hot tub. Whatever you do, I want you to be mentally prepared when I get back. You're about to learn some life-changing truths."

FIFTEEN

"Ladies and gentleman, we have begun our initial descent into Phoenix," came the voice over the PA system. "Please place your seat backs and tray tables into their upright and locked positions, and fasten your seat belts."

Amanda opened her eyes and sat up. After an eleven-hour flight from London to Los Angeles, she had drifted off on her flight from L.A. to Phoenix. She buckled her seat belt, rubbed her eyes, and opened her window shade. She gazed down at the desert landscape. Almost three months in Europe had done her wonders, but it was great to be back.

"Coming or going?" the woman beside her asked.

"Coming back," Amanda said, smiling at her. She was usually a gregarious conversationalist on flights, but she'd been too tired to strike up a conversation earlier. "I've just been in Europe for about three months."

"Wow. Alone?"

"Yeah," Amanda said. "I had the time of my life. I went from London to Rome and saw just about everything in between."

"I'm jealous," the woman said. "But I think I'd be too afraid to do anything like that. So what prompted it? Did you plan it for a long time?"

Amanda shook her head. "Actually, no. It was kind of just a whim. Let's just say I needed a break."

"That's some break."

Amanda laughed. "Yeah, I wasn't really planning on staying that long. Actually, I didn't have much of a plan. I was just having too much fun to come home. There's so much to see and do. So much great food to try. It's pretty overwhelming."

"Sounds like an unforgettable trip."

"Oh, yes," Amanda said with a smile, brimming with memories. More memories slid into her consciousness when she looked down and saw the Phoenix Mountains, where she and Shaun used to ride their mountain bikes. She enjoyed the memories and then released them effortlessly; she had forgiven Shaun, and in that forgiveness she had been able to let him go.

The plane landed, and Amanda sent her dad a text message to let him know. She picked up her bags from the carousel and then walked outside. A few minutes later, her father rolled into view.

He bounded out of the car. "Amanda!"

"Hi, Daddy!" she cried out.

They embraced, and she wiped away a few tears.

"So glad to have you back," he said. "I've missed you. And worried about you."

"It's great to be back. I missed you too."

They loaded Amanda's bags into his Toyota 4Runner and headed toward her house.

"So, I've enjoyed your e-mails," he said. "It was fun to track your trip. Sounds like you had a blast."

"It was just what I needed," she said. "I can honestly say I'm completely over my guy troubles."

"I don't know about that," he laughed. "They'll just be starting when you get married someday."

"You know what I mean," she said with a grin.

He stroked her hair affectionately. "Yeah, I do. I'm glad to hear it."

"The first couple of weeks were hard," she said. "But after a while I was having so much fun, it all just kind of faded away. Once I hit Granada, in Spain, and saw the Alhambra, I was in heaven. You got my pictures, right?"

"Sure did. They were great."

"I've got more pictures than I could ever share on Facebook," she said. "You should have seen it all, Daddy. It was magical. Notre Dame Cathedral in Paris was awe-inspiring. But that was nothing compared to St. Peter's Basilica in the Vatican. It was so beautiful, I cried. The pictures don't do it justice. And the blooming orange trees and curving cobblestone streets in Seville filled up an entire flash drive. The Coliseum in Rome just about made my heart stop. I spent an entire day there."

Amanda gushed the whole way home about the landmarks and attractions and museums she'd visited. Her father sounded thrilled when he noted how beautiful and peaceful she looked—how she radiated a carefree freedom he hadn't seen in her since before her breakup with Shaun. Amanda knew she was truly back, in more ways than one.

Her father dropped her off at her house and carried her bags inside for her. "So I'll see you at dinner tonight, right?" he asked.

"Of course," she said, hugging him again.

"I'll be sure to dust off the slideshow projector," he teased.

After he left, Amanda plopped onto the couch. She lay resting for several minutes, letting it sink in that she was really back. Then she retrieved her cell phone from her room to listen to her voicemails.

SIXTEEN

Shaun was reading in the living room when Stewart's family got home from the soccer game.

"Have you eaten lunch?" Stewart asked him.

"Yes, thank you," Shaun responded.

"I'm going to grab a bite. Then I'll meet you in the library."

Thirty minutes later Stewart joined him.

"All right, strap yourself in," Stewart said, grinning, "because we're about to go deep. The fourth law is the Law of Alignment. *It states that everything you think, say, and do must be in alignment with what you want to manifest. The more closely your beliefs are aligned with truth, the greater power you have to manifest your creations.*

"This law is about purifying your beliefs. A Conscious Creator can't manifest his desires without a completely aligned belief in himself and in what he wants to create. Your belief must be pure, whole, and undefiled by contradictory beliefs and desires. You must be single-minded in order to gather the power you need to accomplish your vision. And your beliefs must be aligned with truth.

"Most people are misaligned in almost every aspect of their lives. It's what I call being 'fractured.' They say one thing and do another. Their fearful beliefs do not match their boastful words. The word 'integrity' comes from the Latin *integer*, meaning whole or complete. So fractured people are out of integrity with themselves. I don't mean that they're immoral or unethical, but rather that they simply can't gain the power they need, because of their misalignment. The more fractured you are, or the less whole and complete you are, the less power you have.

"One of the most common and crippling ways we become fractured is by confusing *beliefs* with *truth*. We tend to assume our beliefs are true. A belief is an acceptance that a statement is true. But when we examine the word 'belief,' we find within it the word 'lie.' Beliefs are not necessarily true. In fact, more often than not, they are *not* true. Any given belief may contain many, few, or no elements of truth. Regardless, it is separate from truth.

"Truth, on the other hand, is independent of belief. It is absolute, objective reality. There is no element of lies in truth.

"Your paradigm is composed of the sum total of all your beliefs. The truer your beliefs, the more empowering your paradigm. The more false your beliefs, the more disempowering your paradigm.

"You lack power to the extent that your beliefs are false. The more aligned your beliefs are with truth, the greater power you have to manifest a positive, purposeful reality. False beliefs slow down the gestational period of creation, which you'll learn about later. They hamper your creative power and lead to poor and mixed results.

"One of the major differences between unconscious creators and Conscious Creators is their understanding of beliefs and truth."

Stewart walked to his desk, brought back three worksheets, and handed one to Shaun, which Shaun read.

Unconscious Creators

- **False Belief #1:** They assume their beliefs are truth.
- **False Belief #2:** They don't believe they can alter what is true. Since they assume their beliefs are truth, they are powerless to alter their reality.
- **Action Mode:** They create from existing evidence and personal belief of what they can or cannot do.
- **False Belief #3:** They feel that because they never have, they never will.

Conscious Creators

- **Truth #1:** They see the limitations of beliefs and strive to upgrade their beliefs to truths.
- **Truth #2:** They give themselves permission to change their reality.
- **Action Mode:** They create what they want without any existing evidence.
- **Truth #3:** They feel they can manifest creations from what they have never done before.

Shaun finished reading and looked up. "Makes sense," he said.

Stewart nodded and continued. "Unconscious creators are trying desperately to hike up the mountain of accomplishment. But they're burdened with so many false beliefs, which are like rocks in their backpack.

"I've been examining my own false beliefs and those of other people for many years. Here are the top thirty limiting beliefs I've encountered."

He handed Shaun the second worksheet.

Top 30 Limiting Beliefs

- I can't do it.
- I'm not worthy.
- I'm not worth it.
- I'm too old.
- I'm too young.
- My body can't do that.
- I don't know enough.
- I'm not special.
- No one loves me.
- No one listens to me.
- No one cares about me.
- I can't change.
- Change is hard.
- I'm scared.
- That's not in my nature.
- I'm not good enough.
- I'm stupid.
- I'm too fat.
- There's too much risk.
- It'll take too long.
- It'll cause family drama.
- I don't deserve it.
- I can't afford it.
- No one will help me.
- It's never been done before.
- I'm not strong enough.
- I don't have the energy.
- I don't know how to do it.
- I'm too busy.
- God doesn't want me to.

Shaun smiled and nodded periodically as he read the list.

"Any of those sound familiar?" Stewart asked.

"Most of them," Shaun admitted.

"Well, you're not alone. Everyone is limited by false beliefs to one extent or another, either the ones on this list or an infinite number of others. Thankfully, the Law of Alignment gives you the consciousness and tools to overcome them.

"This is vital because conflicting beliefs severely limit your power. In *Think and Grow Rich*, Napoleon Hill teaches that your brain is both a transmitter and receiver of energy. He says the subconscious mind is the 'sending station,' which broadcasts thought, and the creative imagination is the 'receiving set,' through which the energies of thought are picked up. I wholeheartedly believe with him that the human brain emits frequencies, just like radio waves, which pass through the ether and are picked up by other human brains and even affect physical matter.

"Holding conflicting beliefs makes us transmit mixed signals, which can even stop transmission entirely. Conflicting thoughts essentially cancel each other out and obstruct the Law of Attraction.

"This is why, when I taught you the Law of Attraction, I stressed that most of the work of manifestation is completely in your *thinking* rather than your *actions*. When you have paid the price to eradicate enough of your negative beliefs, and your beliefs are more closely aligned with truth, you then have the power to take a desire that is in alignment with your purpose and call it into physical creation."

"So how can I actually do that?" Shaun interjected.

"We'll get there," Stewart assured him. "But first I want to make sure we've laid a solid foundation for the principle of alignment.

"What's fascinating about human nature is that although few people truly are aligned and in integrity with themselves, we have a natural urge to be aligned. Ever heard of the term 'cognitive dissonance'?"

"I vaguely remember reading something about it in the one psychology course I took in school," Shaun said.

"Cognitive dissonance is the feeling of discomfort that results from holding two conflicting beliefs," Stewart explained. "Studies have shown that when we have conflicting beliefs, desires, or behaviors, we have to change something to eliminate the dissonance. In other words, we seek some form of integrity. For example, suppose a person is torn by the desire to smoke and the fact that smoking is unhealthy. To eliminate the cognitive dissonance, he would have to align one with the other. In other words, either he'd have to tame his desire to smoke, and align that desire with his desire to be healthy, or he'd have to align his health beliefs with his desire to smoke by convincing himself that he can beat the odds or that smoking will be worth the costs.

"Human beings have an astounding capacity for self-deception. In most cases, we'll accept and align with false beliefs in order to eliminate cognitive dissonance. We deceive ourselves in a desperate desire to get rid of the discomfort of conflicting beliefs and to feel whole. Russian novelist Leo Tolstoy nailed this concept when he wrote—listen carefully to this now—'The majority of men do not think in order to know the truth, but in order to assure themselves that the life which they lead, and which is agreeable and habitual to them, is the one which coincides with the truth.'

"Self-deception explains every conflict in the world, from global wars to bitter partisanship in politics to the internal battles you fight in your head every day. It explains why people hold so tightly to beliefs that are so clearly at odds with truth. For example, it explains the woman who stays in an abusive relationship because she's convinced herself that she doesn't deserve anything better. It explains the man who abuses her—he convinces himself that she deserves it, that he's somehow justified. It explains the pride-driven workaholic who misses the best years of his children's lives, then tells himself that he works to provide for them. There are countless examples.

"Some people will defend these false beliefs to the bitter end of their lives, because they can't bear the thought that they could be wrong. More precisely, when we're self-deceived, we can't bear the thought that we're responsible for our own emotions, actions, and results. Self-deception is the cause of blame and victimhood, such as the abusive man blaming his actions on the fact that he was abused as a child.

"Again, the point is that we have an internal mechanism that drives us to integrity or some form of internal consistency. We can't stand not being consistent, so we'll move heaven and earth to be consistent, even if it means deceiving ourselves and rejecting truth. We become very selective about our perceptions in order to prop up our false beliefs. We see what we want to see in order to live with our false beliefs. Once we accept a false belief, all evidence points to that belief being true. This self-deceiving mechanism is extremely effective. It's why most people have such little power and why so few consciously create.

"It also explains why the Law of Attraction 'doesn't work,' as skeptics perceive. In truth, the law works one hundred percent of the time—but for most people, it works to their detriment. People burdened by false beliefs attract poor and negative results.

"In your case, for example, you accepted the belief that passion doesn't pay the bills. The evidence you've seen and accepted in your life appears to support that belief, despite all the evidence to the contrary. For a long time you didn't even see evidence supporting the belief that passion can pay the bills. Am I right, or am I assuming too much?"

"Yes, you're right," Shaun admitted.

"It's more common than not," Stewart said. "I'm not immune to self-deception either. I struggled with it a lot in my life before I discovered the six laws. When my father left my mother and me when I was thirteen, I adopted a lot of false beliefs. I believed that I had caused him to leave, that he didn't love me, that I couldn't trust or depend on anyone. Those false beliefs led to a lot of anger and feelings of inadequacy, which is why I fought so much in high school. Thankfully, my mentor, Wayne, gently and lovingly guided me to create new beliefs. And in creating those new beliefs, I gained the power to change my life. And I'm still purging limiting beliefs.

Every day. And every time I do, I become more aligned and more able to harness more power to create.

"See, that's the greatest tragedy of self-deception, of being fractured: It relinquishes our power—the power we need to accomplish vision, to create the life we want, to create businesses and products and services that change the world.

"Fractured people have given their power away through victimhood, blame, or negativity, or through simply not having a clear vision. Just like me, when I was in high school: I had no power to create a life of joy, because I had given that power away to my father and everyone else who was, I felt, out to get me.

"Let me elaborate on one point—I want to clarify this idea of the loss of power: No one can actually take our power from us. We simply relinquish our power and then point to people and circumstances as the reasons why we've done so. But in reality, our power is waiting for us to take back anytime we want it.

"So fractured people say they want a life of meaning, but their subscription to *People* magazine says otherwise. They say they want to accomplish their goals, but they trash themselves with self-criticism. In one breath they say they want more privileges, and in the next they defend their inadequacies. Nothing is ever their fault. They want that promotion and raise at work, then they blame their boss or their coworkers when they don't get it. They talk about starting a business, but they never start it, supposedly because of the poor economy or some other excuse.

"People say they want world peace, and then they get angry when they get cut off on the highway. Submitting to that anger gives their power away, because it's not aligned with their desire for peace. They say they want more money and prosperity, but then they envy and criticize their prosperous neighbors. They hold conflicting beliefs: On one hand, they think money is the root of all evil, but on the other hand they want more of it. They say they really want to read and learn more, then they spend all their spare time watching TV and lurking on Facebook. They say they want a healthy marriage, then they secretly indulge in pornography. Their actions don't back up their supposed desire.

"What these people really mean is that they want their desires to materialize *with minimal effort*. They're not willing to pay the price.

"Think of a car that's out of alignment. If you take your hands off the steering wheel, it's going to veer off the road. You may have your GPS set to a particular destination, but if you let your misaligned car have its way, you'll never get there. You have to take control of the steering wheel. Even better, you can get to the root of the problem by taking your car in to the shop and getting it aligned so it's easier to steer. Fractured people are driving a misaligned car with their hands off the steering wheel. Then they get frustrated when they don't arrive at their destination.

"The real challenge with this fourth law is that most of our misaligned desires and contradictory beliefs originate in our subconscious mind. So most people aren't even aware of their existence, let alone aware of how to conquer them. Most cognitive neuroscientists believe that ninety-five percent of our thoughts, emotions, and learning occur without our conscious awareness. As Duke psychology professor Dan Ariely put it, 'We are pawns in a game whose forces we largely fail to comprehend.'

"The subconscious mind is an incomprehensibly powerful force. It can work either for or against you. The Law of Alignment helps you harness the mind's power to achieve your vision and goals. Fortunately, there are ways to expose our subconscious thoughts to the light of consciousness so we can align them with our conscious desires.

"One of the best things to do in aligning with your conscious desires is to pay close attention to your emotions. Certain emotions serve as clues that we're out of alignment. Emotions are also critical because the Law of Alignment isn't just about what we think, but also about how we feel. Negative emotions take power away from the Law of Attraction and cause us to focus on negativity. We attract both what we think and what we feel. Desiring something you want while feeling the emotions from not having it will repel your desire. Ultimately, you must learn to align your thoughts with your feelings.

"Here's a worksheet I created to help me identify misaligned beliefs and desires," Stewart said, handing Shaun a sheet of paper.

Emotional Clues Worksheet

The following emotions are clear indicators that some aspect of your life is misaligned or that you hold a false belief. For the next month, write down every time you feel any of these. Then ponder on how you may be misaligned. Write down the source of misalignment.

- Fear
- Anger
- A feeling of being victimized
- A sense of being imprisoned, inhibited, restricted, trapped, controlled
- Helplessness, powerlessness
- Defensiveness
- Frustration, stress

- Confusion, a feeling of directionlessness, dissatisfaction
- A sense of defeat or disempowerment
- A sense of being disheartened or unmotivated
- Guilt, shame
- Jealousy, envy, resentfulness
- Depression, despair, misery
- Uncertainty about choices and desires, indecision
- Addiction
- Cynicism, pessimism
- A feeling of inferiority
- A feeling of being rejected, unloved
- Embarrassment

When Shaun finished reading and looked up, Stewart asked the same question he had asked earlier: "Any of these sound familiar?"

"Just about every one of them," Shaun admitted once more. "In fact, some of these emotions are exactly what brought me here. I've been feeling so frustrated that I haven't had time to cook and create new recipes. I've been unmotivated to go to work. I've felt trapped by the desire for money, benefits, and security. I didn't want to admit it to myself, but deep down I felt guilty when I took this job in Seattle. I knew, at least subconsciously, that I was doing it mostly for the money and not for a higher purpose. Although at the time I didn't even comprehend passion like I do now."

Shaun was also thinking of Amanda and his feelings of anger, jealousy, inferiority, and rejection, but he didn't share this with Stewart.

"Well," said Stewart, "the good news is that you know *why* you're feeling these emotions. Most people don't even know that. And, of course, the reason you know why is because you've finally detailed your vision.

Without that vision in place, you wouldn't be nearly as conscious of why you've been feeling this way. Like most people, you'd just feel a general sense of dissatisfaction. And, also like most people, you'd jump around from job to job, from project to project, trying to alleviate the dissatisfaction. Actually, as you've already admitted, you did do that—by taking this job. Most people keep using the same failing strategies in hopes that they'll create different results—even though we understand this behavior as being the definition of 'insanity.'

"That's precisely why *vision* must come before *alignment*. Your vision is the standard with which everything in your life must align. Without that standard, you're a rudderless ship on the wild ocean of your subconscious.

"You can't become happy by simply trying to escape things that make you unhappy. You can't grow corn just by deciding you don't like carrots. Happiness comes from living your purpose and serving others through your purpose. You become happy not by avoiding unhappiness, but by pursuing a clearly defined and noble purpose. Happiness is a by-product, not a goal."

Stewart grabbed a book and opened it to a marked page.

"I've taught you some things from Viktor Frankl. Here's another passage I love, from *Man's Search for Meaning*." He began to read:

> *Success, like happiness, cannot be pursued; it must ensue, and it only does so as the unintended side effect of one's personal dedication to a cause greater than oneself or as the by-product of one's surrender to a person other than oneself. Happiness must happen, and the same holds for success: you have to let it happen by not caring about it. I want you to listen to what your conscience commands you to do and go on to carry it out to the best of your knowledge. Then you will live to see that in the long*

run—in the long run, I say!—success will follow you precisely because you had forgotten to think about it.

Stewart put down the book and continued, "So your job is to apply the Laws of Attraction and Purpose to create a vision, to take accountability for your reality, and to choose empowering thoughts. Then you must align all your thoughts, desires, beliefs, emotions, and actions with your vision. The vision must consume you. You must be fiercely vigilant about the thoughts you entertain. You must become the gatekeeper of your thoughts. Where your mind frequently travels, your body is certain to follow. The purer your belief, the more your physical creations will reflect your spiritual vision. And the faster and more effortlessly they will manifest into reality."

Noting a puzzled look on Shaun's face, Stewart paused. "I've given you quite a bit to digest. What are you thinking?"

"Well, I get how our emotions are indicators of misalignment when they come as a result of our own actions," Shaun said. "Like me feeling frustrated about not being able to cook, when I'm the one who took the job that prevents me from having more time to cook. But what about the emotions that arise when other people do things to us? I mean, I understand that I can choose how I *respond* to emotions, but I don't really feel as though I have the power to choose my emotions in the first place. Stuff happens and emotions just come up. If someone were to hit me and I got mad, or someone called me stupid and I felt hurt, would that really mean I'm somehow misaligned?"

"There is a powerful way to handle negative emotions that arise from the actions of others," Stewart said, "and that is to first recognize the people to whom you've given your power—anyone who pushes your buttons or frustrates or upsets you in any way. Then accept those people as your teachers. Understand that the buttons they've pushed are *your* buttons. You, not the other person, are the one who is upset. Ask yourself what higher law you have to learn.

"More often than not, when we're hurt by what other people say about us, it's because there's some truth in their words, and by addressing this truth, we can regain our power. As Carl Jung said, 'Everything that irritates us about others can lead us to an understanding of ourselves.' Being criticized is such an excellent opportunity to address cognitive dissonance in our lives, because it makes it easy to identify this dissonance. It's like clashing musical notes that are really easy to pick out in an otherwise beautiful piece of music."

Shaun thought suddenly of how he had felt when Amanda broke up with him. He didn't feel like discussing it with Stewart, but he knew Stewart was right. There *had* been truth to Amanda's words, difficult though they were to hear. He hadn't been living his passion. He had been afraid to commit.

Silently, he thanked her for teaching him. The silent surrender didn't immediately eliminate the pain, but it did give him power to address the cause of the pain. He knew now that these were his issues rather than anything Amanda had done to him, and that he could control them.

"I think I'm beginning to understand," Shaun said, "at least in principle. I have my vision; now I need to focus on it. Think about it. Align all my thoughts, desires, beliefs, and actions to it. When negative emotions arise, I need to analyze them to find a source of misalignment.

"But how do I actually do it? I mean, it's one thing for me to recognize when I'm misaligned. But it's quite another to actually get aligned."

"Very true," Stewart agreed. "It's simple to understand, though not easy to apply. Everyone picks up false and limiting beliefs throughout their life. Being conscious about them is half the battle. The other half is to reprogram your mind with new beliefs to replace the old ones.

"But that's where it gets deep. I use a process to do this, but I don't want to teach it to you just yet. I've taught you a lot today, and I don't want to overwhelm you so much that you miss the importance of the process. I've got a few more exercises that will help you digest everything I've taught you so far and start working on it. I want you to spend the rest of the afternoon and evening working on these exercises. Then, in the morning, I'll teach you the deeper reprogramming process. What time does your flight leave?"

"Not until four in the afternoon," Shaun said.

"Good. We'll have time. Tomorrow morning you're going to learn how to reprogram your mind to align with your vision. This is where the rubber meets the road—where you start gathering power to attract your desires."

"Well, can I cook for you guys in exchange for all your help?" Shaun asked, smiling.

"I wouldn't turn that down for anything," Stewart said, returning the smile. "You got yourself a deal."

* * *

Readers: *The Conscious Creator's Reparadigming Journal* has a series of powerful exercises to help you identify and replace false beliefs. Download a digital copy for free, or order a hard copy at www.ConsciousCreatorBook.com.

At this point, Stewart has taught Shaun four of the Six Laws of Conscious Creation. They are:

The First Law of Conscious Creation: The Law of Attraction

You attract into your life whatever you think about the most. Your dominant and persistent thoughts eventually manifest as physical reality.

The Second Law of Conscious Creation: The Law of Purpose

For you to achieve your highest potential, your desires and actions must be manifestations of your True Self and True Purpose. Your True Self embodies the highest, most accurate truth from which you can create at your greatest potential. Conscious Creators know who they are and what they were born to accomplish.

The Third Law of Conscious Creation: The Law of Choice and Accountability

Your perception of reality is a choice, not a condition, and your experience is your creation, whether you realize it or not. The more accountability you take for your reality, the greater power you have to change it.

The Fourth Law of Conscious Creation: The Law of Alignment

Everything you think, say, and do must be in alignment with what you want to manifest. The more closely your beliefs are aligned with truth, the greater power you have to manifest your creations.

SEVENTEEN

"So yesterday we talked about how we get misaligned and fractured thanks to false and limiting beliefs," Stewart began the following morning. After gassing up Shaun's car, they had enjoyed a hearty breakfast, prepared by Shaun, and were again comfortable in the library.

"To get aligned and gain power, you have to uproot your false beliefs and replace them with true and empowering beliefs. To do this, I use a simple yet extremely effective three-step method. I call it the Belief Breakthrough Process.

"I use the term 'reparadigm' to describe this process. A paradigm is a set of beliefs, or a certain perception of the world and your place in it. Your paradigm determines your actions. The sum total of all your false and limiting beliefs drastically impacts your paradigm. And you must 'reparadigm' to align with your vision of your True Self and True Purpose. Reparadigming is the process of consciously selecting beliefs that support what you want to manifest. It's a lifelong search-and-destroy mission; you systematically uproot all the falsehoods that are sabotaging your results.

"The process may seem so simple that you may discount it. Shaun, what I do in my home and heart using this process has had far more impact on my life than anything I've ever done in a boardroom. The inner work I do with this process is precisely what has lead to the external creation of my business. Getting aligned in here"—he pointed to his head—"has given me the power to align ideas, relationships, and materials out in the world to achieve my vision. So my advice to you would be, do not treat this lightly," Stewart admonished.

"I won't," Shaun said. "I promise."

"Good. The three steps in the Belief Breakthrough Process are to recognize, replace, and reinforce. We've talked about the first step, *recognize,* which is simply to become consciously aware of areas of misalignment in your life. False, limiting, negative, contradictory beliefs are like weeds in the garden of your thoughts. If allowed to grow, they choke out the good seeds and stifle the plants that would bear the fruits of your creation. You have to be a protective gardener to uproot the weeds and cultivate your true, empowering, positive, and aligned thoughts and beliefs.

"I've already given you one tool to help you do that: the Emotional Clues Worksheet. Another tool is to keep a Belief Breakthrough Journal."

Stewart took a small notebook from his pocket and handed it to Shaun.

"Keep this with you at all times," he said. "Anytime you catch yourself thinking negative and limiting thoughts, write them down immediately. Pull those weeds up at their roots, from the depths of your subconscious mind. Then explore them and try to identify the false assumptions and beliefs underlying them. Write down those false beliefs—as concisely as possible. Write down how they manifest in your actions. Analyze how they hinder you. Dig deep into your past to identify their point of origin—where you took on the beliefs. Exposing them to the light of consciousness is often enough to overcome some of the minor ones.

"But the deeply rooted beliefs need the next step: *replacement.* Once you have a clearly defined a false belief as it pops up in front of you, you're going to create a 'belief-replacement manifesto': a declaration of intentions, opinions, objectives, or motives. A belief-replacement manifesto is specifically designed to attack that false belief and replace it with one that is in alignment with what you want to create. For example, you've struggled with the belief that passion doesn't pay the bills, that it leads to insecurity. Your belief-replacement manifesto could be something like 'My passion is the purest indicator of my gifts and purpose. Security and prosperity come from living my passion and purpose. I create the most value for others when I'm living my passion. I follow my passion without hesitation and follow through with integrity.'

"That's just one example of how you can deal with one false belief. You'll want to go through this process with every other false belief you identify. Just like trading in a used car for a new one, you upgrade from a lower truth to a higher truth—one belief at a time. Assimilating and living truth is a lifelong quest, not a one-time event or something that goes away overnight.

"Once you have developed your reprogrammed beliefs, your next step is to *reinforce* them by repeating your manifestos at least three times a day, out loud, for at least thirty days. The new beliefs will start crowding out the old.

"Think of your beliefs as deep ruts in a dirt road. Ruts are created over the years as thousands of cars drive over the same roads. It rains and the roads get muddy, and the ruts get even deeper. Thoughts, beliefs, and habits are no different. The longer and deeper we've held a belief, the harder it is to break it. You have to choose a different track to drive on—you have to create a new path for your thoughts to travel.

"It can be extremely hard to get out of the deep grooves. But these methods, if applied consistently, will do it for you. At first it will seem just kind of technical, like you're just going through the motions. But over time you'll really experience belief breakthroughs. It will start clicking for you. Negative thoughts will still arise, but instead of caving in to them, you'll start laughing at them and immediately repeating a manifesto.

"As you strive to increase your integrity, your bad habits suddenly become more and more uncomfortable until you hit the tipping point and give them up for good. Things that you once found irresistible become distasteful, then intolerable. As you fill your life with light, darkness flees."

Stewart paused for a moment, then continued. "So I've dumped a lot of theory on you. I'd like to make this more real for you. Are you willing to be vulnerable and open with me?"

"Uh, sure," Shaun said.

"I want to go deeper into your belief that passion doesn't pay the bills. I want you to tell me more about your father."

"Well, I think I've already told you all there is to know. He always talked about living passionately, and he jumped from business to business and project to project in search of his passion, but we always struggled financially. He could never get ahead. Nothing really ever stuck for him. And he and my mom fought about it a lot."

"When was the first time you remember your parents fighting about this?" Stewart asked. "I want to locate the specific point of origin for your belief. When did you decide that your father was a bad provider and that you needed a job to be secure—that security was more important than passion?"

Shaun pondered this for several minutes while Stewart waited patiently. Suddenly, a distinct memory surfaced for Shaun.

"I was eight years old. My dad had quit another job and arrived home in the early afternoon. I remember my parents fighting. My mom was crying. I could tell that she was scared. I think they had some big bills coming due, and she didn't know how they were going to pay them. She yelled at him for a while, and he just sat there. I just remember him saying something like 'I'm sorry, but I just can't do it anymore. I'm just not passionate about it.'

"That upset my mother even more. She kept lecturing him about all the things she did even though she wasn't passionate about them. I remember her saying, 'Why can't you just keep a job like other people and give your family the security we need?' I guess he got tired of it, because he got up and walked out.

"When he left . . . ," Shaun started to say, but then he choked up. He composed himself and continued, "When he left, my mother sat down at the kitchen table, put her face in her hands, and started crying. I remember feeling so worried about her and about their marriage. I hugged her. She said, 'Shaun, someday you're going to become a man and have a family. And there are just things you have to do to be responsible. You'll have bills to pay. I want you to always remember this: Keeping your family secure is the most important thing you can do.'

"And from then on," Shaun said, "I've always been suspicious of my father's thoughts on following passion. And that was reinforced throughout my life every time my mother would say, 'Passion doesn't pay the bills.'"

Stewart nodded thoughtfully. "So what did you decide for yourself that day?"

"I decided that I needed to have a stable job and that that was the most important way to be a responsible man."

"And is that absolutely true?" Stewart asked gently. "Based on your experience over the past few months of doing this work with me and going through your struggles at work, have you learned anything that contradicts that belief?"

"Absolutely," Shaun said.

"And what is that?"

"Well, I've come to realize that there's more to life than just job security. I've learned that a stable job can be stifling. I've learned that I have specific gifts that I'm not using and that I should be using. I've learned that I come alive when I cook and that nothing else I've ever experienced can match that feeling. But I still don't know if I can make a living doing it."

"Well, you'll find out soon enough," Stewart said. "But for now I want you to focus on that feeling. You've experienced both worlds now: a secure job you don't enjoy and a passion that makes you come alive. Which world do you choose to live in? Do you want to continue pursuing money and security, even if it means stifling your passion? Or would you rather live from passion, even if it means sacrificing security?"

Shaun thought for a moment, obviously torn. "Well, I know I want to always feel like I do when I cook. But do I really have to give up security to do that? Is there not a way to do both?"

Stewart smiled and said, "There you go. Now you're learning. That was a trick question. Let's go even deeper. Is it absolutely true that living your passion leads to financial insecurity and that you must choose between passion and security?"

"I don't think so," Shaun said. "But I still struggle with it after seeing the example of my dad for so many years."

"Is your dad the only example you have to look at?"

"No," Shaun admitted. "There's you. You've made an incredible living by pursuing your passion. And my uncle Frank loved his career."

"Can you think of anyone else?" Stewart said. "Think of the most influential, prosperous, and famous people in the history of the world: Bill Gates, Steve Jobs, Thomas Edison, Oprah Winfrey. Do you think they became who they are by sacrificing passion for security?"

"No," Shaun said.

"Do you think it would have been the 'responsible' thing for Steve Jobs to have ignored his passion to create technology products and instead work in a regular job his whole life?"

"Of course not," Shaun said. "In fact, I think that would have been irresponsible. He had too much to offer. He never could have contributed as much to the world as he did if he hadn't started Apple."

"And is it any different for you? Are your gifts and purpose any less important than those of Steve Jobs?"

"I guess it depends on what I do with them," Shaun said.

"Exactly!" Stewart exclaimed. "So the question is, what are you going to do with them? What is the *responsible* thing to do with them?"

A light clicked on in Shaun's head. "The responsible thing would be to develop them and serve others with them. And it would be irresponsible of me to do anything less."

"Now we're getting somewhere," Stewart declared. "I have another question about your father. Do you think he really pursued his passion?"

Shaun thought long and hard. "You know, I don't think he's ever really found his passion. I think he's always been looking for it. He always talked about it being important. But I don't ever remember him explaining what his passion is."

"And do you think he wasn't a good provider *because* he pursued his passion and True Purpose?"

"No," Shaun realized. "I think he struggled with providing precisely because he wasn't sure what his purpose *was*. I think that's why he did so many different things."

"Do you think he could be prosperous and secure if he were more clear on his passion and purpose and if he truly pursued them?"

"Without a doubt," Shaun said. "He's very smart. He's driven to succeed. He's not lazy, by any means. He's great with people. He's a quick learner. It always seemed as though success really could be just right around the corner for him."

"Okay, so let's circle back now. Shaun, is it true that passion doesn't pay the bills?"

"I think it depends on how you apply it," Shaun said. "And I think it's absolutely possible for anyone to earn a living doing what they love to do."

"Good," Stewart said. "And is it true that being a responsible man and provider means taking a 'secure' job?"

Shaun shook his head. "No."

"I want you to do something now," Stewart said. "I want you to picture that eight-year-old boy watching his mother cry and interpreting from her pain and worry that passion doesn't pay the bills. What do you want to say to that boy, knowing what you know now?"

"I want to tell him that passion *can* pay the bills. I want to tell him that he was born for a purpose and that the responsible way to live is to find and pursue that purpose no matter what." Shaun leaned forward, getting more and more excited. "I want to tell him that living from passion creates the greatest security in life. I want to tell him to never give up on his passion, even when it's hard. I want to tell him that applying his gifts to serve others is the path to prosperity.

"And I want to tell him that his mother loves him more than anything and that she believed what she said—she only wanted to protect him and take care of him. I want to tell him that it was just her belief, and it may not have been true, but she was doing the best she could in her circumstances. I want to tell him that his father is a good man with a good heart, that he just hasn't found the right path yet."

Stewart honored Shaun's vulnerability with a respectful moment of silence. Then he said, "Excellent work, Shaun. Do you have total confidence that you can live that way now?"

"Honestly, I'm not sure," Shaun said. "In this moment I feel like I can, but I know things will probably change when I go back to Seattle and get back into my same old routines."

"I understand," Stewart said. "But you will not be able to progress until you can believe in yourself, until you have faith that you can create income and security from your passion. I want you to state the new belief—the one that is going to replace the old, false beliefs."

"Okay," Shaun said, fumbling for the right phrase. "Umm, I think I can earn income and create security by living my passion."

"No, not 'I think,'" Stewart interjected. "State it like you mean it."

"But I don't know if I can really believe it," Shaun said. "At least not yet."

"But that's exactly the point," Stewart exclaimed. "You have to believe it before you can live it. That's the only way it works. You can't prove false beliefs wrong by holding on to those beliefs and trying to live differently. You have to replace the false beliefs with true ones first, and then your actions naturally follow your beliefs."

"But how do I know what beliefs are true or not?" Shaun asked.

"A more useful way to think of it is to ask which beliefs will serve you and your purpose," Stewart countered. "Whichever belief you choose will *become* true in your actions. You've lived according to a particular belief for your entire life, and it hasn't gotten you to where you want to go. That's the beauty of this process: *You get to choose your beliefs.* And the beliefs you live become true, at least through the actions you take. Choose and live different beliefs, and you'll take different actions, and you'll therefore attract different results.

"See, trauma like you've described—that experience with your parents—introduces cognitive dissonance and opens the door for new beliefs. The new beliefs can either be more limiting or more empowering. Unconscious people gravitate to the lower, limiting, false beliefs. As a Conscious Creator, you get to choose upward into higher, truer, more empowering beliefs. Your mind cannot live with both of those types of beliefs. As a Conscious Creator, you get to choose up instead of down. You get to choose the higher beliefs that will serve you better. You get to choose the beliefs that, if reinforced, will crowd out the false beliefs."

Stewart grabbed the notebook in which Shaun had written his vision and held it up. "So answer this: Which belief serves this vision and purpose best?"

"That I can create income and security from my passion."

"There you go," Stewart said. "Now state it like you mean it."

"I *can* create income and security from my passion," Shaun pronounced more loudly.

"No, restate it more powerfully," Stewart prodded.

Shaun thought for a moment, then confidently declared, "I live my passion courageously because that is the path to security and prosperity."

"Now we're talking," Stewart said. "Now, from here you must reinforce that belief by repeating that manifesto three times daily for at least thirty days." He paused to let the impact of the exercise soak in. Then he asked, "Shaun, how do you feel now?"

"Stronger. More powerful." Shaun struggled for just the right word. "Lighter, somehow. Like I've released a burden."

"And what about your life has actually changed in the last few minutes?" Stewart asked.

"Nothing, I guess, other than my thinking."

"Precisely," Stewart said. "You just did more for your future with this Belief Breakthrough Process than you might have accomplished with any other effort, no matter how hard you were to work. Can you see how this process will be valuable for you?"

"Definitely," Shaun said, examining the Belief Breakthrough Journal. "I'm excited to use it. I'm sure I have plenty of other false beliefs getting in my way."

"Do this exercise, and do it consistently," Stewart charged. "You won't really comprehend the power of this law until you experience it for yourself. And, as I've mentioned, that is the result and real benefit of living the Law of Alignment: You gain the *power* necessary to attract relationships and resources and to manifest your creations.

"You give away your power when you allow the negative words and hurtful actions of other people to erode your beliefs. You give away your power when you surrender to temptations and addictions unworthy of your True Self and True Purpose. You give it away when you engage in self-criticism. You give it away when you cave in to discouragement. You give it away when you don't act on your promptings to follow purpose. You give it away when you enroll people in your stories of victimhood so they can support and justify your inadequacies.

"The more aligned you become, the more power you gather back from all these sources you've given it away to. Fear melts away. You're more confident and at peace. You gain greater clarity on your vision and purpose. You stay more motivated and inspired. You begin attracting the right relationships and circumstances to achieve your vision. As you stop spending time and energy on distractions, you have more time and energy to focus on your mission. You become filled with a light that's almost tangible. And as you shine your newfound light onto the path before you, new opportunities are revealed. You start seeing what your next step should be. You stop questioning your intuition and start following it fearlessly."

Shaun pondered this for a few minutes.

"So this light you speak of, of knowing what your next step is," Shaun said, "I think that's what I need most right now. It seems to me that my next step should be to quit my job and open my restaurant. But I don't have enough money and experience to do it. Is that just fear talking? Am I misaligned to think of those limitations?"

"Not necessarily," Stewart said. "Achieving an ultimate vision takes time and experience. There's a natural process that must be allowed to unfold. I'll explain that more when we get into the final law. I'm not going to teach you that law now, but to prepare you for it, I have a challenge for you—what I call the Thirty-Day Creation Challenge. I've given it to dozens of people, and it works. It will help you see that you can earn income by living your passion."

"Sounds like fun," Shaun said. "What does it entail?"

"It's very simple. Your challenge is to simply earn as much money from your passion as you can within thirty days. So, in your case, you have thirty days to earn money by cooking, even if it's just a dime here and there. You're not starting a formal business. You're just doing whatever you can to make money. Then, write down all the lessons you learned from the process. Watch what unfolds; pay attention to any doors that open. Follow the paths that are revealed. I guarantee you'll find something."

"Sounds easy enough," Shaun said.

"Yes, most people are surprised to find that it's much easier to earn money from their passion than they ever thought," Stewart concurred. "But the real magic happens *after* the thirty days—*if* you keep going, if you keep applying the lessons you learn to create at even higher levels."

"I'm definitely in," Shaun declared, his head already spinning with ideas.

"I look forward to hearing your reports. And I also have another assignment for you. While you're doing the Creation Challenge, I also want you to live the Law of Alignment by using the Belief Breakthrough Journal. Specifically, within the next month I want you to identify ten limiting beliefs and replace them with empowering beliefs that serve you and your purpose.

"I really want you to understand that this is not a one-time deal. Reparadigming and replacing false beliefs is a lifelong discipline. I've come a long way since I started doing this, but I still catch myself thinking negative thoughts and acting from false beliefs from time to time. Over the years I've uprooted thousands of false beliefs using this process."

"When do I get to learn the final law?" Shaun asked.

"Work through the Belief Breakthrough Process and do the Creation Challenge for the next month," Stewart said. "Then we'll connect on a phone call so I can teach you the final two laws."

Stewart stood up, and Shaun followed his lead.

"Thanks again, Stewart."

"You're very welcome, Shaun. Keep up the work. I know you're going to experience some major breakthroughs."

Shaun went to the guest room and lay down on the bed, his head spinning with all he'd learned. He felt like a tremendous burden had been lifted from his shoulders. He felt an internal wholeness he'd never felt before. The joy of being released from false beliefs was overwhelming and deeply satisfying. He wanted more of that feeling. He realized he had a little time before he needed to leave for the airport, so he opened his Belief Breakthrough Journal and began working on the exercises.

* * *

Readers: Visit www.ConsciousCreatorBook.com to get your own Belief Breakthrough Journal, which is found within *The Conscious Creator's Reparadigming Journal,* and to join the Thirty-Day Creation Challenge.

EIGHTEEN

"I've had employees lie to me before," Brad said, "but this is the first time anyone's ever admitted it."

It was Monday morning. Shaun had returned to Seattle the previous evening and had just told Brad the real reason why he'd missed two days of work. As part of his alignment process, he knew he needed to do whatever he could to make it right with Brad.

"I'm truly sorry," Shaun said. "It is inexcusable, and I won't blame you if you fire me. Whatever you do, I sincerely hope I can regain your trust."

"Shaun, you've done a great job for us. Our clients love you. You've really helped them out and saved them money. So now you've put me in a tight spot." Brad stared out his window, sighing long and deep.

Shaun sat listening, prepared to accept whatever Brad decided.

Brad suddenly laughed, catching Shaun completely off guard. "Cooking, huh? I knew you enjoyed it, but I never would have guessed that anyone could get that engrossed in cooking, of all things. I can't stand being in the kitchen."

"You know," Shaun said, "I wouldn't have imagined something like this either, until just a few weeks ago. It's been a slow awakening process."

"All right," Brad said. "I appreciate you telling the truth. I'm not happy about your dishonesty, but all things considered, I think we can work through that. My bigger concern is where this leaves us. I mean, do you even want to be working here? It sounds like you'd rather be cooking for a living."

"I won't lie," Shaun said, "I do think cooking for a living is where my newfound passion is leading me. But I'm not anywhere close to being ready for that. I really do enjoy providing innovative solutions for our clients. I'd prefer to stay."

"Tell you what," Brad said, "we'll keep you on. But how would you feel if we gave your new clients to Sarah? I'd have to retract the raise, but your hours would be more reasonable."

Shaun hesitated. He hated giving up the raise, but he knew what he needed to do. It was time for him to prove that he had chosen passion over money and security, and the reduced work hours would give him more time for cooking. "That's totally fine. I really appreciate it."

"Let's see how it goes for a month. And I don't want you skipping work to cook anymore. You can do that in your spare time."

"That's more than fair," Shaun said. "Thank you so much. I promise it won't happen again."

"I'd appreciate that," Brad said. "Now, I think you've got a lot to catch up on. Let's get to it."

Shaun was pleased with the arrangement. "Thanks again," he said. As he opened the door to leave, he was struck by an idea. He knew this was a risky time to make a request, but he shut the door again and turned around. "Brad, you said you hate being in the kitchen. So what do you do for lunch?"

"I usually just eat out," Brad said. "Why?"

"If I bring you lunch tomorrow, will you eat it?"

"I guess," Brad said, shrugging his shoulders.

A bit nervous, Shaun rushed his next sentence. "And if you like it more than what you've been eating for lunch, will you pay me to bring you lunch to work every day? It won't cost you any more than you're paying now."

Brad laughed. "You've got guts, Shaun. Sure, what the heck. Let's see what you got."

"Great. Plan on it tomorrow. Any special requests?" Shaun said with as much calm as he could muster.

Brad shrugged his shoulders. "Surprise me. I'm easy."

As soon as he left Brad's office and closed the door, Shaun pumped his fist into the air, thrilled for his first Creation Challenge opportunity.

He worked late that night, catching up on his work and meeting with Sarah to make the transition. On the way home he stopped by the grocery store to pick up a few items for Brad's lunch. He ate a quick dinner, then started preparing lunch for the next day. He had been thinking about it all day and had decided to make Greek pitas along with a quinoa salad with apples, walnuts, dried cranberries, and gouda. He packaged the meal in a plastic container and fell into bed, exhausted, by eleven.

Shaun bounded out of bed early the next morning, excited to give Brad his lunch. He showered, dressed, and then left for work an hour early. He still had quite a few things to catch up on. He was the first one in the office, and he worked diligently until Brad arrived an hour and a half later.

"Good to see you, Shaun. I hear you arrived early," Brad said as he walked by Shaun's desk.

Shaun smiled. "I'm just grateful to be here at all. Hey, I left your lunch in the fridge."

"Lunch?" Brad raised his eyebrows. "Oh, yeah, I'd forgotten all about that. Well, good. I look forward to it."

"You'll let me know what you think?"

"Sure."

"And you promise to tell the truth?"

"Of course. Just like you did," Brad said, laughing and winking.

Shaun grinned sheepishly as Brad walked away. He continued working but had a hard time focusing. He was worried that Brad wouldn't like his lunch.

At twelve thirty, just as Shaun was about to break for lunch himself, Brad rushed into his office. He was chewing. "Shaun, if this is your way of getting back into my good graces, it totally worked," Brad said. "I have no idea what's in here, but this is one of the best salads I've ever eaten. Absolutely fantastic."

"I'm so glad to hear it," Shaun said.

"And these pitas are super," Brad raved. "I'm definitely in. I'll pay you to bring me lunch. Name your price."

"I hadn't really thought that far," Shaun fumbled. "I don't know. Does $10 a day sound fair?" He was amazed by his boldness, and he worried that he'd asked for way too much.

So he was amazed when Brad responded, "That's more than fair. You got yourself a deal. At least, as long as you keep producing food this good."

"Done," Shaun said almost too quickly, shaking Brad's hand.

"Now, if you'll excuse me," Brad said, "I've got more of your food waiting for me."

After Brad left, Shaun leaned back in his chair, put his hands behind his head, closed his eyes, and basked in the moment. *Could it really be this easy?* he thought. He'd been hungry before he'd spoken with Brad, but he forgot all about it as his mind raced with ideas for future lunches. He opened a new document on his computer and started typing menus. After he'd planned out the next month, he realized his lunch hour was over. He saved and closed the document and got back to work.

Shaun was on the phone thirty minutes later when Jeremy, a coworker, approached his desk. Jeremy waited for Shaun to finish his call and hang up.

"Hey, Jeremy, what's up?" Shaun asked.

"Brad told me you're going to bring him lunch every day, and he shared a bite of your food with me. I want in too."

"Seriously?" Shaun asked.

"Are you kidding me?" Jeremy said. "I already spend that much eating out, but I've never had anything that good for lunch. It's a no-brainer."

"All right," Shaun said in wonder.

He left work by six and rushed to the store to pick up everything he'd need for the next few days. After eating dinner he lost all track of time, preparing the following day's lunch.

At lunchtime the next day, Brad again raved about his meal. Jeremy was just as pleased.

Before the day was through, word had spread through the office and two more people had asked to be included in the lunchtime deal. Shaun was astounded. Cooking came so easy to him that he found it almost impossible to imagine his service was really that valuable.

Ten dollars per day per person, for four people, five days a week, he calculated mentally. *And it will probably cost me around $5 per meal. So $20 a day net, a little more than $400 a month. Not too shabby for hardly doing anything at all.*

That week was the most fulfilling week of his life so far; each day he got compliments on his meals. The next week, when two more coworkers as well as two people from an adjoining office asked to be included on his list, Shaun was forced to get serious about systems. He found that although preparing the food was easy, it became complicated to figure out packaging and to transport all the food to work. He still kept up on his work, and he was careful not to spend work time on his side project. But every spare moment was spent preparing food and experimenting with packaging options. He dropped into bed late each night, exhausted but thoroughly satisfied.

As he lay in bed that Friday night, the thought that had been nagging him subconsciously since he'd started his Creation Challenge finally surfaced: *I could quit my job and earn a living just cooking lunches for office workers.*

Immediately, as the thought arose, he was gripped by fear, and the thought was overwhelmed by competing thoughts. *You're crazy. You've just gotten lucky. You'll give up a guaranteed paycheck and great benefits. You'd have to get a business license, and find a commercial kitchen. It would be way too complicated and expensive, and you have no experience with entrepreneurship. You know you'll fail, and where will that leave you? You'll have to go crawling back to Brad, begging for a job.*

Unconsciously, Shaun entertained the negative thoughts for a while, and the fear deepened. Then it dawned on him what was happening. He laughed out loud. *Those are just beliefs,* he told himself. *And I get to* choose *my beliefs.* He realized that the fear he felt was an indication of false beliefs, and he knew he had some work to do.

The next morning Shaun took a break from cooking to go hiking near Mount Rainier. He hiked to an overlook, got comfortable, and took his Belief Breakthrough Journal out of his backpack. He spent several hours going deep inside himself, identifying false beliefs, and then completing the exercises in the journal. He developed a replacement manifesto for each false belief he'd identified. Stewart had asked him to go through the process with at least ten false beliefs, but more than two dozen flowed onto his pages as he examined his past openly and free of self-deception, justification, and rationalization.

By the time he finished, he felt the same as he had after Stewart had taken him through the process for the first time: light, free, mentally clear, confident, empowered. He read and reread his new belief manifestos, soaking up their power:

- "There's no such thing as failure. There is only learning."
- "I can make my passion profitable."
- "Living my passion and purpose creates the greatest security in my life."
- "My food is valuable enough to charge for it and worth at least what I'm asking for it."
- "I spontaneously act on the right opportunities."
- "I am the master of my fear."
- "I love my fear because it tells me what I need to do."
- "I am worthy of success."
- "I make time to invest in my passion."
- "I serve people when I honor myself."
- "I stand in my power when I share my purpose with others."

He felt intoxicated by gratification and accomplishment—and above all, hope—as he considered what doors these new higher beliefs would unlock for him. *Stewart has been able to accomplish so much by reparadigming,* he thought, *and I know I can do the same thing. I know I can open my restaurant and share my passion with the world in a way that will make me wealthy and happy.*

Shaun shut his journal, closed his eyes, and basked in the sunlight and the experience. He'd never been much of a praying man, but he felt compelled to offer a vocal prayer of gratitude to his Creator, with whom he felt closer than ever before. His words were awkward at first, but it just felt right to give thanks. "Thank you for giving me the ability to create. Thank you for my power to choose. Thank you for all the wonderful opportunities available in my life."

Still basking, he ate his lunch and turned his thoughts to business ideas. He still wasn't settled on pursuing the idea he'd had the night before, but he knew that if he didn't pursue it, it wouldn't be because of fear or the prospect of difficulty. Shaun knew he'd never be satisfied until he built the restaurant he'd created in his vision. But he also realized that it was going to take some foundational steps. Still, he never wanted to lose sight of that ultimate vision. He'd also brought his written vision with him, so he took it out and read and reread it several times. He spent the rest of the afternoon exploring and enjoying nature while pondering his vision, imagining it in great detail.

When he got home that evening, he wrote his vision and newly created belief-replacement manifestos on a large poster board and posted it on a conspicuous wall so he could read them often to reinforce the new beliefs.

The next morning, after eating breakfast, he called his father.

"Hello?"

"Hey, Dad. It's me," Shaun said.

"Hi. How's your job treating you? And how is Seattle?"

"Just fine. Things are going really well. I'm working on a new project, too. I'll tell you about it sometime. But that's not what I called about."

"What's on your mind?"

"Dad, I've been thinking about a lot of stuff lately. About how you and

Mom used to argue about money, and about Mom's frustration with you not settling into a job."

"Oh, Shaun. You know we've always loved each other through it all, right?" asked his father.

"Of course," Shaun said. "But what I'm really getting to is that I've had my own feelings and beliefs about everything, and I want to own up to them. To tell you the truth, I've always kind of sided with Mom. You know, about the whole 'Passion doesn't pay the bills' thing and wanting more security. I've harbored resentment toward you about it, and I'm calling to apologize for that."

"Shaun," his father lamented, "I'm sorry. I really wish I had been a better provider for you. God knows I've tried."

"No, no, it's okay, Dad. I don't want you to feel bad about anything. I understand now. I love and appreciate you so much. I couldn't have asked for a better father. I know you tried. But you did more than try; you succeeded. You succeeded in transferring your passion and teaching me the importance of following passion. I now know how hard it is to follow passion and push through fears. Despite any failures you think you might have, you were always fearless. And your example has been invaluable. Please forgive me for my negative thoughts and feelings."

There was silence down the phone line for a moment. "Oh, Shaun, there's nothing to forgive. I'm so proud of you. I know you're going to accomplish far more than I ever have."

"Well, I don't know about that," Shaun said. "But no matter what I do, always know that you've been a fantastic teacher, and I love you more than anything."

"I love you too, Shaun."

After they hung up, Shaun again felt an immense joy from letting go of past negativity. He felt so empowered by his newly discovered ability to choose his feelings and beliefs.

The next two weeks passed in a blur of working through the days and cooking in the evenings. By the end of the month, Shaun was cooking lunches for fifteen people, in both his office and other offices in the building. And through it all, he continued his alignment work with his Belief Breakthrough Journal. He felt it becoming easier for him to arrest negative thoughts, track them to their source, and reparadigm with the exercises. Above all, he was happier than he'd ever been. He missed Amanda, and his social life had suffered, but the fulfillment he felt was worth it. He was thrilled to share his results with Stewart.

NINETEEN

"So how did your reparadigming work go?" Stewart asked. It had been a month since their last meeting, and they were reconnecting over the phone.

"It's been totally amazing," Shaun said. "I feel so free and alive. So . . . so . . ."—he grasped for the right word—". . . *unburdened*. I feel like I can accomplish anything. Like nothing can hold me back."

"That's what I like to hear," Stewart said. "And I trust you came up with some belief-replacement manifestos and wrote them down?"

"Oh, dozens. Here, let me read them to you." He read Stewart his manifestos. "And I've been reciting them three times a day. I can feel power gathering every time I do it."

"Excellent work," Stewart said. "You've done a really great job of making those positive, compelling, and empowering. Keep it up. Like I told you, the Belief Breakthrough Process will have more impact on your success than anything else you could ever do.

"But let's get to what I'm sure you're bursting at the seams to tell me. How'd your Creation Challenge go? Did you make any money?"

"Eighteen hundred and ninety-three dollars total, to be exact," Shaun crowed triumphantly. "Nine hundred and thirty-five dollars net, after expenses."

"Fantastic!" Stewart exclaimed. "I'm thoroughly impressed. How'd you do it?"

"It was actually pretty simple," Shaun answered. "In fact, it has almost seemed too easy. That even worries me a bit, like it's too good to be true. But I can't argue with results. All I've been doing is cooking lunches for some coworkers and a few other people in my office building. I really didn't even do any marketing. I started with my boss, and he raved about my food so much that word spread. I'm now bringing lunch every day for fifteen people. It's actually getting pretty hectic to manage it all."

"I love it," Stewart said. "Simple, meets an obvious demand, easy to do on the side. And what did you learn?"

"Oh, I don't know if we have enough time on this call to download everything I've learned," Shaun said. "This has seriously been the most amazing month of my life. More than anything, I've learned that I really can do this; I really can earn income by living my passion. I don't know that cooking lunch for office workers is the next million-dollar business idea, but I'm sure I could even replace my current income doing it.

"Of course, I still have a lot to learn about running a business before I'd be comfortable quitting my job. But I've learned tons about business in these past thirty days. I've had to get smart about developing systems to manage all this in my free time. And I'm improving things every day."

"That's the first lesson of business anyway," Stewart said. "Nobody has all the answers, and you've got to just keep innovating and learning. It can be a trick to stay profitable through mistakes. But you've got the right attitude, and with your new beliefs you'll learn quickly and adjust, no matter what temporary failure you experience."

"So I don't suppose you could help me create a plan for moving forward," Shaun asked hesitantly, not sure if it was the right time to ask.

"Well, we'll get there," Stewart said. "But first I'd like to teach you the final two laws: the Law of Faith and the Law of Gestation.

"*The Law of Faith states that Conscious Creators work with complete faith that they can manifest their desires, and they act on that faith with courage, despite having little or no evidence from their past accomplishments.*

"Conscious Creators understand that they have the power to manifest anything in which they have complete faith. I define 'faith' as a complete trust or confidence in any belief or truth. Note that faith can work either for or against you. People who believe they're fat and put faith in that belief will develop conscious and unconscious behaviors that will surely manifest fatness. Whatever you put your faith in can manifest. Therefore, Conscious Creators are vigilant about what they choose to put their faith in.

"This is a step above the Law of Attraction. In fact, this gives final power to the Law of Attraction. It's about more than just *thinking* about your goals. It's *believing* with unwavering faith that you will achieve them, long before you achieve them. And that's the secret.

"Everything a Conscious Creator manifests was not there beforehand. Conscious Creators know that all new, improved, or expanded creations will be manifestations that previously never existed. They have faith in their truth—that it will manifest without any evidence, other than the fact that they have manifested intentionally before. Conscious Creators know they can manifest anything they choose to believe.

"Unconscious creators operate from the perspective of 'I'll believe it when I see it.' Conscious Creators operate from the opposite perspective: 'I'll see it when I believe it.'

"Shaun, I know this sounds strange, but it is absolutely true. When you upgrade your belief system, you'll have no prior evidence to back it up. You must act in courage and accept with complete faith that this new statement is your new truth.

"Everything you want to create in your life isn't there yet. You're going to create manifestos that are going to feel like a lie, because you have no prior evidence of their being manifested in your life. The secret is that you must move forward in faith, despite the lack of evidence. You must move forward believing with courage that it is your new truth—and taking action on the new belief, despite the fact that it hasn't been your belief before now. Believe that your restaurant is a reality, and live that belief *without doubt,* and it will come to pass.

"You've already experienced this, in fact. A month ago you believed it was not possible to make money by living your passion. But then you reparadigmed that belief and boldly proclaimed that you could. Now, thirty days later, you're nine hundred and thirty-five dollars richer, not to mention wiser. You created that wealth with no prior evidence that you could do so. Imagine what you can create by intentionally replacing fear with a greater goal that you choose to put faith in!

"Living the Law of Faith requires commitment. As Roy H. Williams wrote, 'A committed person paints a picture of a possible future and then works to bring that picture to life. They see it before it happens. They believe it before it's true. And they take action.' For example, as a Conscious Creator you might look at an acorn and see a forest, then act with diligence to make that forest come to pass. No one else around you will see what you see. People will think you're crazy. But that's precisely why visionary, committed entrepreneurs are compensated so highly: They see things that others can't see and take the leap of faith. They commit time, energy, money, and other resources to projects, without any external guarantee that those projects will pay off. Their faith manifests their vision.

"Speaking of vision, that's the fundamental discipline of this law: consistently visualizing your desired outcome. When I gave you the exercise to create your vision of your ideal self, I was laying the foundations for the Law of Faith. Because it's not enough to just write down your vision one time, file it away, and forget about it. You must revisit your vision daily. High-performing athletes use this technique all the time. Ever heard of Peter Vidmar?"

"I don't think so," Shaun said.

"He's a gymnast who understands the Law of Faith. In 1983 he was a student and gymnast at UCLA, along with Tim Daggett, his workout companion and another famous gymnast. Peter was obsessed with becoming the best gymnast possible. He and Tim were chosen to be on the U.S. team for the 1984 Olympics.

"They would practice six to seven hours a day. Peter would always be the last one in the gym. He would be sore and tired. He would have blisters. But he used visualization to get through the most difficult days.

"He would imagine this: There are fifty thousand people in the auditorium. The Chinese team is just ahead of the American team. He is the last American gymnast to perform. If he gets a perfect ten on the pommel horse, the U.S. men's team will win the all-around gold medal in men's gymnastics for the first time.

"He imagined seeing the judge salute him, and returning the signal to begin his routine. He saw himself—in intricate, frame-by-frame detail—mounting the pommel horse and performing his routine flawlessly. He visualized dismounting perfectly and holding up his hands once more.

"He imagined the scorecards raised high above the judges' heads: all perfect tens. He saw the crowd going wild and felt the triumphant emotion. He saw himself standing on the podium to receive his gold medal.

"Day after day, hour after hour, Peter Vidmar would visualize that entire scenario to push through pain and to work longer and harder than anyone.

"Fast-forward to the 1984 Olympics in Los Angeles. The exact scenario that Peter had envisioned unfolded. He was the last gymnast to perform. If he got a perfect ten, the U.S. would win the all-around gold medal.

"When asked later if he had been nervous, Peter said, 'You know, I really wasn't. I'd done it every day for a year. All I had to do was go out and do what I had seen myself do countless times.' Peter mounted the pommel horse and performed a perfect ten routine to make history, all because he believed before he saw."

"That's powerful," Shaun said in awe.

"I agree," Stewart said. "The human imagination is more powerful than I think any of us realize. Tapping into it even to a small degree will revolutionize your life. If you rely on your five senses alone, you'll do only what you've seen done before. You'll never take the leap into uncharted territory. The key is having absolute, doubtless faith.

"See, this is one major reason why unconscious creators can never manifest what they want: They don't actually have faith that they *can* get what they want. The frequency of desire they transmit with their thoughts is canceled out by their frequency of disbelief."

Shaun nodded. "I've definitely felt that in my own life." He pondered that thought for a moment. "So the one question I have about this law is, does it speed up the process of creation? I mean, I believe I do have absolute faith that my restaurant will become a reality some day. But I don't know when it will happen. Should a specified time line be part of my visualization?"

"Excellent question," Stewart answered. "The short answer is *yes,* living the Law of Faith through consistent visualization will definitely increase your creative speed. But having said that, there's another law at play that must also be understood. This is the sixth and final law of Conscious Creation: the Law of Gestation.

"This is perhaps the simplest law to understand, but it's vital because it gives you the strength to persevere.

"*The Law of Gestation states that there is a natural gestation period for all acts of creation—the greater the goal, the longer the gestation period.* You asked me last month if you should quit your job to start your dream restaurant. That's like a woman who has been pregnant for a month asking if she should deliver her baby immediately. Like babies, dreams and visions must gestate.

"All acts of creation manifest in their own time. When something doesn't manifest on your schedule, it means you have a false expectation and you're out of alignment with truth. In that case, either the creation itself needs more time or you haven't become who you need to become in order to be worthy of the creation. Understand that the gestational period applies both to the creation itself as well as to the creator. For the creation to manifest, the creator must become equal to the creation.

"The gestation period serves two purposes. First, it gives you time to take the practical steps required to achieve the vision. And second, it proves that you'll pay the price. Right now, your restaurant vision is a premature baby. It needs to be protected and fed so it can grow. It needs the nutrients of practical action. You *could* quit your job, but how long would your savings last? Do you have enough money to open a restaurant of this magnitude? Even if you did, do you have the experience to make it successful?"

"No and no," Shaun said.

"Don't get me wrong," Stewart continued, "I'm not saying that it would necessarily be a bad thing if you were to try and fail. I'm simply saying that you must honor the gestation period if you want your creation to manifest according to your vision. And above all, you must first pay the price in your personal development.

"Vision is an incredibly powerful tool, but it is impotent in the absence of action and experience. It pulls you through dark times and keeps you motivated, but you still have to pay the price of any creative endeavor.

"If your dream is worth achieving, then you need the staying power to stick with it regardless of time or obstacles. Most people fail at great ideas because they want it all to happen *now*. They're not willing to pay the proper price for their dream. That's what separates successful creators from failures. With the right expectation, you can stick to the effort required to gestate and birth your creation.

"Now, let's say you do decide to step off the cliff and make your dream happen immediately. You scrounge up the start-up capital from somewhere. And you fail spectacularly. Would that be the end of your vision?"

"Well, I guess it would be the end of that particular attempt at it," Shaun said. "But I could keep trying."

"Exactly," Stewart said. "However you approach it, whether by taking baby steps or giant steps, there will be a predetermined price to pay. The proving grounds of achievement, if you will. Now, after all my business failures, I don't recommend that you take my path and bite off more than you can chew. It's possible to succeed that way, but your chances are poor. Most people get too scarred and burned to ever try again after a major failure, particularly when it involves other people's money.

"So instead of jumping in over your head, my recommendation is that you take your ideal vision, then backtrack to fill in the blanks between where you are now and where you want to go. What would you need to learn in order to run a successful restaurant? How much money would you need to open one? Would there be other ways to start other than a restaurant? There are hundreds of questions you need to answer before you decide where to go from here.

"But ultimately, analysis can take you only so far. The most powerful thing you can do is to just act. Do something, anything—today and every day—that will get you closer to fulfilling your vision.

"See, when they learn the Law of Gestation, a lot of people get discouraged. They see the long, hard road ahead of them. They have a sense of how much time it will take. So instead of nourishing their vision with small, consistent actions, they freeze up and that vision dies in the womb.

"This is an unfolding process. You just take action today, without knowing how it will develop exactly. One step leads to another. Doors open up that you didn't even see before. You follow your bliss and meet people, form new relationships. These open even more doors.

"Here's an analogy: Think of a house. You know that inside the house there's something you want. You open the front door to discover a hall with many other doors. You open one door after another. Some doors are dead ends. Some are traps. But inside others you find clues leading you to what you want. If you keep opening enough doors, you eventually find the right one and get what you want.

"But in life too many people stop opening the doors. They stay trapped in a confining room of their choosing, whether that room represents a job they hate, a bad relationship, or anything else that keeps them from getting what they truly want. They just don't have the staying power to keep going."

Shaun interjected. "Or they don't even walk into the right house to begin with. Like me becoming a CPA, or taking this job for the wrong reasons."

"Right," Stewart agreed.

"Okay," Shaun said, "so—small, consistent actions in the right direction are the key."

"Exactly. You have to trust the process, and you have to persevere. In his classic book *Think and Grow Rich*, Napoleon Hill tells the true story of a man who caught gold fever in the gold rush days and headed west to get rich. He staked a claim and went to work. After working hard for a few weeks, he finally discovered shining ore. But he needed heavy machinery to bring it to the surface.

"So he quietly covered up his mine and went back home to solicit help from family and friends. They returned with machinery and shipped their first car of ore to the smelter. The returns showed that they had one of the richest mines in Colorado. So they kept drilling feverishly.

"But unexpectedly, the vein of gold ore disappeared. They drilled on, but to no avail. They quit digging, sold the land and machinery to a junk man for a few hundred dollars, and returned home. The junk man called in a mining engineer to study the mine. The engineer concluded that the project had failed because the owners were not familiar with fault lines, and he calculated that the vein would be found just three feet from where the family had stopped drilling.

"Sure enough, that's exactly where it was found, and the junk man took millions of dollars in ore from the mine. My point is this: Without knowing or trusting the Law of Gestation, too many would-be creators work hard to uncover their vein of gold, but then stop right before they would have struck it rich."

"Okay," Shaun interjected, "this makes total sense. So what would you say is the gestation period for my restaurant idea? How long do I need to pursue the vision before it becomes a reality?"

"Well, there's no hard-and-fast rule," Stewart said. "It's kind of just something you learn with experience. You should also know that there are ways to quicken the gestation period—for example, the purer your beliefs, the shorter the gestation period. So the Law of Alignment has a direct and immediate impact on this sixth law. The more consistent you are with your alignment and reparadigming work, the faster you'll achieve your goals. Remember that the gestation period is about *creating yourself* as much as it is about manifesting your vision into physical reality.

"Suppose you want to become a millionaire but you have thirty false beliefs preventing you from doing so. Reparadigming one of those false beliefs will not manifest a million dollars overnight. In this case, during the gestational period you will need to reparadigm every false belief that prevents you from achieving your goal. Perhaps these beliefs include 'Money is the root of all evil' or 'Rich people are unethical' and so on.

"Christ spoke of having the faith of a mustard seed. A mustard seed, if planted today, does not bear fruit tomorrow. It first manifests as a tiny sprout. That sprout grows into a bigger plant with its first leaf and so forth. The mustard seed has faith that it will unfold as it was meant to, all in its own time, and you must have the same faith in your vision and yourself.

"See, a major reason why many people don't believe in the Law of Attraction is that they want overnight success without paying the price, doing the work, and waiting patiently for the results.

"You are on a never-ending journey of creation. As you work toward your purpose and uproot your false beliefs, you'll start seeing evidence that *something* is happening, but at first you will not see fruit. You must continue the journey. Improvement does not always manifest in immediate achievement. The seeds of success you plant today must be cultivated and nourished over time. Achievement is often made up of months, years, even decades of trying and failing and manifesting small results one at a time, until eventually your greatest creations grow to fruition and bear fruit.

"In his book *Outliers,* Malcolm Gladwell analyzes highly successful people to learn how they achieved their success. He discovered that they all had one common trait: They put in ten thousand hours of work in their field to become world-class. Ten thousand hours is 'the magic number of greatness,' Gladwell says. Now, if you can work full time on your passion and purpose, that ten thousand hours translates into five years, working forty hours a week. But it took about ten years for most of the people Gladwell studied to master their craft.

"For example, the Beatles played in clubs in Hamburg, Germany, for seven days a week, eight hours a night for several years before making it big. Mozart was a child prodigy who started incredibly young. But he didn't compose his best symphonies until age twenty-one, after he'd been composing for ten years. And when Bill Gates was an eighth-grader, his parents sent him to a private school that had built a computer lab. While other kids were playing sports, Gates lived in that lab, writing code deep into the night, almost every night. He eventually moved to the University of Washington computer lab, where he continued what he calls his 'obsession.' He said it would be a rare week when he wouldn't get twenty or thirty hours of programming in. By the time Gates dropped out of Harvard in his sophomore year to start a software company, he'd been programming continually for seven consecutive years and was way past ten thousand hours."

"Sounds grueling," Shaun said, a little disconcerted. He felt impatient to start living his vision.

"On the contrary," Stewart countered, "it would be grueling only if you didn't enjoy the work. If you're practicing your natural talents and living from passion and purpose, it's a thrill. Especially if you get paid to practice, like you've been doing with the Creation Challenge."

"I guess that's true," Shaun acknowledged. "I said myself that this has been the best month of my life. But does this mean that I won't be able to open my restaurant for five to ten years?"

"Not necessarily," Stewart said. "It just means that no matter how thrilled you are about your recipes now, you've got some recipes in you that you haven't even dreamed of yet that will rock the world. And don't discount the years you've already spent cooking. Just because you've just recently become conscious of your passion doesn't mean you're starting from square one. You've got some business knowledge and experience to gain, but you're already fairly advanced with the cooking."

"So where do I go from here?" Shaun asked. "Any recommendations?"

"Well, it seems pretty obvious to me that you're onto a great idea now," Stewart said.

"Should I quit my job?" Shaun asked.

"I can't answer that for you," Stewart replied. "You'll have to trust your intuition. And you'll get better at hearing and trusting your intuition as you continue your alignment work. What does your intuition tell you now?"

"Well, I hope this isn't just fear," Shaun said slowly, "but something tells me to wait."

"Trust it," Stewart said. "I'm confident that you'll know when it's time. For now, I'd say just keep doing what you're doing. It's working for you. You're progressing. You know you're headed in the right direction.

"But I would also say this: Continue to set bigger and bigger goals. For example, last month you netted almost a thousand dollars. Set a goal to earn two thousand dollars this month. What happens is, your current ceiling becomes a new floor. Your thinking expands. You gain confidence. It becomes easier for you to conceive of even bigger accomplishments. It's just like building muscles: the more you work toward your dream, the stronger you become."

"Sounds like a plan," Shaun said. "I can do this."

"Shaun, listen to me." Stewart paused, as if struggling for words. "I wish I could just open your brain and pour this knowledge into your head, or just inject it into your veins. At the moment, this power is almost incomprehensible to you. I know, because I used to be where you are now. You have the spark of divinity within you. You have been given the power to create. Creation—your ability to manifest your thoughts and vision into tangible reality—is your birthright. But you're just getting a glimpse of what these laws can do for you.

"When you and I first started working together, I tried to convey to you the depth and power of these laws. Empires are created by Conscious Creators using this power. Man's most debilitating problems are solved through this power. Think of the Wright brothers; for years, they were mocked and ignored. Now, because of the power of these six laws to manifest creative vision, we fly around the world, even into space, and think nothing of it. For thousands of years we communicated only in person or by written message, until Conscious Creators applied these six laws to enlighten us with telegrams, telephones, and eventually cell phones, the Internet, Skype, social media. We suffered from plagues and diseases until Conscious Creators experienced Nobel Prize–winning breakthroughs by applying these laws. Electricity was just a natural occurrence we didn't understand until Conscious Creators harnessed it for our homes, buildings, and technology. The Sistine Chapel ceiling was bland mortar until a Conscious Creator applied these laws to make it a masterpiece.

"When you start applying these laws, you'll be like a child learning to walk or ride a bike. You'll be clumsy and awkward. You'll stumble and fall. But the more you live them, the easier it becomes. They'll become ingrained into your soul, a natural part of your life. You'll start dreaming bigger. You'll start manifesting effortlessly. Things that seemed impossible to you before will become easy. What you felt during that experience you shared with me, about creating your latest recipe, will become your default mode rather than a fleeting anomaly. You will get so deeply into the flow that the world will shift to make your vision become a reality.

"It's been said that at the moment of commitment, the entire universe conspires to assist you. This is absolutely true, but I would add the word 'alignment.' Once you commit to and align with your vision in every aspect of your life, nothing can stop you."

Shaun was mesmerized. "That's the kind of life I want to live," he said, his voice full of emotion. "It's exactly what I felt the first time I heard you speak. Somehow I knew I had it in me, and now I know I can do it."

And it's exactly what Amanda saw in me that I failed to see, he thought.

They hung up, and Shaun calculated how he could double last month's earnings from his side project.

* * *

Stewart has taught Shaun all Six Laws of Conscious Creation. They are:

The First Law of Conscious Creation: The Law of Attraction

You attract into your life whatever you think about the most. Your dominant and persistent thoughts eventually manifest as physical reality.

The Second Law of Conscious Creation: The Law of Purpose

For you to achieve your highest potential, your desires and actions must be manifestations of your True Self and True Purpose. Your True Self embodies the highest, most accurate truth from which you can create at your greatest potential. Conscious Creators know who they are and what they were born to accomplish.

The Third Law of Conscious Creation: The Law of Choice and Accountability

Your perception of reality is a choice, not a condition, and your experience is your creation, whether you realize it or not. The more accountability you take for your reality, the greater power you have to change it.

The Fourth Law of Conscious Creation: The Law of Alignment

Everything you think, say, and do must be in alignment with what you want to manifest. The more closely your beliefs are aligned with truth, the greater power you have to manifest your creations.

The Fifth Law of Conscious Creation: The Law of Faith

Conscious Creators work with complete faith that they can manifest their desires, and they act on that faith with courage, despite having little or no evidence from their past accomplishments.

The Sixth Law of Conscious Creation: The Law of Gestation

There is a natural gestation period for all acts of creation—the greater the goal, the longer the gestation period.

TWENTY

"Mr. Wilcox would like to see you in his office," Sherry, the receptionist, told Shaun on a Thursday afternoon.

Shaun wondered if he'd done something wrong. It had been a month and a half since he'd skipped out of work, but sometimes he still felt as though he were still on probation. He knocked on Brad's door, and Brad called, "Come in."

"Hi, Shaun." Brad gestured to a chair, and Shaun settled in. "I've been really pleased with your work since our last chat," Brad said. "You've really stepped up. And I know you've been cooking lunches for people on the side. I appreciate that you haven't let that interfere with your work. And of course, I've really loved your lunches."

"Thank you," Shaun said, relieved.

"Hey, I've got a favor to ask," Brad said, switching gears.

"Sure, anything."

"I just got off the phone with an old college friend," Brad said. "I haven't seen him in a while. He wanted to get together with me, so I invited him and his wife over to our house for dinner Saturday. They're both gourmets, and I'd like to do something special for them. I know this is really short notice, but I was hoping I could get you to cater dinner for the four of us. I'll pay your expenses plus $400 to do it. You can come early and prepare everything in our kitchen if you'd like."

Shaun stammered, "Sure, I'd like that."

"I thought you'd say that," Brad said. "I really want to impress him, and I know you can do it. I want you to go all out and spare no expense."

"Any special requests for the menu?" Shaun asked.

"Nah, I trust you for that. Surprise us."

Shaun left Brad's office in a daze. Brad's offer for one meal would pay him double what he was grossing daily now that he was bringing lunches for twenty people. It would be almost a week's worth of side income for just a few hours of planning and cooking.

On Saturday morning, Shaun spent an hour and a half finalizing his menu for the evening, then headed out to shop. By the time he'd finished, after visiting a dozen specialty shops, it was two o'clock in the afternoon. He rushed home, showered, put on some nice clothes, and loaded his car with ingredients. He arrived at Brad's house by four o'clock.

"Come on in, Shaun," Brad's wife, Rachel, said when she welcomed him at the door. "Follow me." She guided him to the kitchen, and he placed the bags he was carrying on the countertop.

"Hey, Shaun," Brad greeted him, walking in from the living room. "Need help bringing anything in?"

"Actually, that would be great," Shaun said. "I've got quite a few bags."

After all the bags were set on the counter, Rachel showed him around the kitchen. "Would you like any help?" she asked.

"Oh, no," Shaun said, "but thank you. You guys go do whatever you need to do. And you know where to find me if you need me."

Ten minutes later his ingredients were spread across the counters and he was engrossed in his work. He'd arrived later than he intended, and he knew he had to hurry to start serving by seven o'clock. After his experiments of the previous nights, he'd decided on a fried artichoke appetizer with whipped ricotta, pickled tomatoes, basil, and garlic aioli, followed by grilled pepper salad and then his lamb chop recipe—the same masterpiece he'd missed work to create a month and a half earlier.

As Shaun worked, he settled into an almost trancelike state that he'd been experiencing more and more frequently. Time melted away. Any outside observer would have seen him working fast and furious, his hands almost a blur as he chopped and sliced, stirred and mixed. But to Shaun it felt almost as if he were moving in slow motion. He intuitively anticipated every move. No motion was wasted, and his efficiency would have made any expert chef envious.

He was putting the finishing touches on dessert, a hazelnut cake with chocolate gelato and espresso crème, when the doorbell rang. Brad and Rachel met their friends at the door, then escorted them to the back patio, where they'd prepared candlelit tables.

Rachel came back to the kitchen. "How's it coming?" she asked.

"Just finishing up," Shaun said.

"No rush, but we're ready anytime."

"I'll have your appetizers out in just a couple minutes," Shaun said.

He finished the cake, then placed the appetizer plates on a tray and carried them outside. He was surprised to discover that he recognized Brad's friend.

"Shaun," Brad said, "I want you to meet our friends Aaron and Ilana Weiss."

Shaun set his tray down and shook hands with the Weisses.

"Aaron and I were roommates at Duke," Brad said. "He was always the smart one."

"I wouldn't say smart," Aaron deflected. "Just too shy to get out much."

"Don't let him fool you," Brad said. "Aaron graduated at the top of our class with a dual MBA and law degree. And he's made more money in business in the last fifteen years than I'll ever make in my life."

Aaron was clearly embarrassed by the focus on him.

"Aaron," Shaun interjected, "don't I know you from somewhere?"

"You do, indeed," Aaron said. "You teach a cooking class at the youth home."

"Yes, that's it!" Shaun said. "I've seen you there a few times. Are you a volunteer too?"

"Well, I suppose you could say that. I do my best to help out where I can," Aaron said.

"Don't let him fool you with his modesty," Rachel said. "Aaron's generous donation helped to start the home, and he's our number one donor."

Aaron shot Rachel a look, and he quickly moved on, saying, "And what about you, Shaun? Accountant and business consultant by day, famous chef by night?"

Shaun blushed. "Certainly not famous, but I do love to cook."

"We'll try not to judge your food too harshly," Aaron joked drily. "But from what I've tasted during your classes, I'd have to say I'm looking forward to it."

"Thank you," Shaun said, placing the appetizers in front of each of the four diners.

"Speaking of your classes," Aaron continued, "I can't thank you enough for your contribution. You've really made a difference for our kids. I've overheard many of them talking about how much they enjoy your class."

"That's great to hear," Shaun said. "I've thoroughly enjoyed teaching the class."

Shaun retreated to the kitchen to prepare the salad plates. He returned several minutes later, anxious to hear their reaction to his appetizer.

"Shaun," said Ilana, "that was wonderful."

"Agreed," Aaron added warmly. "It was superb."

Shaun glowed.

Brad turned to face him. "You should know that means a lot. Aaron and Ilana haunt the best restaurants in town. You can't get Aaron to spend a dime on anything else," he teased, "but his pocketbook is a bottomless well when it comes to food."

"So glad you liked it," Shaun said, replacing their appetizer plates with salad plates.

"And what have we here?" Aaron asked.

"Grilled pepper salad with arugula, almonds, melon, and harissa yogurt," Shaun said, not quite succeeding in hiding his pride.

"You're sure you're not a famous chef? Or perhaps you're just following the recipes of some famous chef?" Aaron said with a twinkle in his eyes.

"Nope," Shaun said. "These are all original recipes I've created myself."

"I'm quite impressed," Aaron said.

Shaun exited again to prepare the main course. He returned just in time to hear Brad gasp in disbelief, "Sixty-three *million?*"

Aaron nodded.

Shaun tried to be as inconspicuous as possible as he retrieved their plates, but he couldn't help but overhear their conversation.

"I'm hoping you can help me figure out what to do with it," Aaron said. "I've got a few ideas, but I thought you may have some as well."

"Wow," Brad said. "I'm still trying to wrap my brain around it. I knew your company was doing well, but I had no idea it was doing *that* well."

"We've been blessed," Aaron said.

"And you know what Aaron always says," Ilana added. "'It's not ours.'"

Shaun carried his tray to the kitchen and returned with the main course.

Aaron interrupted their conversation. "Shaun, you're two for two. That salad was amazing. And I've got a feeling you're going to knock this main course out of the park."

"I hope you like it," Shaun said. "It's my favorite recipe, if I do say so myself. It took me weeks to perfect."

He set the plates before each of them and stood back to watch. He knew he should give them privacy, but he couldn't help it—he *had* to see their first reaction.

Each person took a bite as Shaun held his breath.

Aaron closed his eyes and chewed slowly. After several moments, he opened his eyes and looked at Shaun. "Shaun, this is divine."

Ilana chimed in, "He's right, Shaun. I've never tasted lamb this good—and I've tasted plenty of lamb, believe me."

"Agreed," Aaron said. "And this potato salad would win prizes."

Brad and Rachel beamed with pleasure. Shaun bowed awkwardly and went back to the kitchen.

Aaron looked after him thoughtfully.

Shaun checked in on them periodically as they finished their meal, just looking through the sliding glass door so as not to interrupt their conversation. When they had all finished, he returned with dessert.

"Oh, my," Aaron exclaimed as Shaun placed a plate of cake in front of him. "Let me guess: hazelnut?"

"You got it," Shaun said and smiled.

"One of my favorites," Aaron said. "I'm beginning to suspect Brad set this up to make me weak and write him a big check."

"Hey, now," Brad said, "I'm just trying to take good care of an old friend."

Once again, Shaun couldn't resist waiting to watch their reactions, and again he was not disappointed as they raved about the tastes and textures. He left them to finish their conversation and went back to the kitchen to clean up.

An hour later, just as Shaun was putting the last dish away, the diners came back into the house. He could hear them talking as they walked down the hall to the front door.

"I'll ask around," Brad said, "and see what I come up with."

"I appreciate that," Aaron said.

As they were saying their good-byes, Shaun heard Aaron say, "Is Shaun still here?"

"Yes," Rachel responded. "He's in the kitchen."

"Give me a minute, will you?" Aaron said to Ilana, and a moment later he appeared in the kitchen. "Shaun," he said, "Thank you so much for that wonderful meal. You have a gift."

"Thank you, Aaron," Shaun said.

Aaron took a card out of his wallet. "I want you to give me a call on Monday morning. Will you do that?"

"Sure," Shaun said, wondering what it was about. He suspected Brad had convinced Aaron to work with their firm.

Shaun packed his car and drove home. His meal had been a hit, and he couldn't be happier.

TWENTY-ONE

It was Monday morning. Shaun was working at his desk, trying hard to concentrate. He leaned back, rubbed his eyes, and sighed. After his frantic but satisfying Saturday, he had still had to cook twenty lunches on Sunday. His late nights and long hours of involvement with his extracurricular activity were catching up with him. He knew something would have to give soon, especially if he picked up more customers. He hadn't even been marketing his lunch project, mostly because he worried he couldn't keep up with the demand. But he also was concerned about upsetting Brad.

At the thought of Brad, suddenly Shaun remembered that he was supposed to call Aaron Weiss. He grabbed Aaron's card from the drawer, lifted the phone from its cradle, and punched in the number.

"Aaron Weiss."

"Hi, Aaron. This is Shaun Porter—I work for Brad Wilcox. We met at his house on Saturday."

"Of course. How are you, Shaun?"

"I'm just fine, thank you. You asked me to call you . . . ?"

"Yes, thanks for remembering," Aaron said. "I'm eager to speak with you. Can we meet for lunch sometime this week?"

"I'd love to," Shaun said, assuming that Brad had arranged the connection for business purposes. "How does tomorrow look for you?"

"That will be fine. Can you meet me at Dahlia Lounge on Fourth Street at twelve thirty? My treat."

"I've got it scheduled," Shaun said. "See you then."

Since this was going to be a business meeting, Shaun knew he would need to buy Aaron lunch from the business account instead of letting him "treat." Regardless, Shaun was looking forward to meeting with Aaron. He'd been impressed with him on Saturday. If nothing else, it would be a great opportunity to learn from a successful man.

At lunchtime, he caught up with Brad. "Hey, Brad. Did you ask Aaron Weiss to meet with me about business or something?"

"No," Brad said. "Why?"

"Before he left your house on Saturday, he asked me to call him today. I spoke with him earlier, and he wants to meet me for lunch tomorrow."

"Huh. I have no idea what that would be about," Brad said with a curious frown.

"I hope it's okay," Shaun said quickly. "I accepted because I assumed you had arranged it."

"Of course," Brad said. "Don't worry about it. He's looking for some new investments, and I told him I'd ask around. But I don't know why he'd ask to meet with you, so now I'm just as curious as you are. Let me know how it goes."

"Sure thing," Shaun said.

Tuesday afternoon found Shaun waiting in Dahlia Lounge. Aaron joined him a few minutes later, and they were escorted to a table.

Aaron ignored his menu and waited for Shaun to decide. Shaun tried to bottle his curiosity as he looked over the menu.

"You must try their salmon," Aaron recommended.

"I'll take your word for it," Shaun said. They ordered, and Shaun waited expectantly.

"You must be wondering why I asked you to meet with me," Aaron said.

"Yes," Shaun said. "I thought it was something you and Brad had arranged, but he said he knew nothing about it."

"I was very impressed with you on Saturday," Aaron revealed. "My wife and I are regulars at the finest restaurants in town. We're no strangers to fine food, but your meal rivaled anything we've ever tasted."

"Thank you so much," Shaun said.

"I'm very curious to know why you're working as a CPA and consultant when you clearly have a phenomenal gift for cooking," Aaron said pointedly. "I'm a big believer that people should develop their gifts. I'm not saying you don't have a gift for accounting, but you, my friend, have a talent that needs to be shared with the world, not just a few people on Saturday-night catering gigs."

Of all the possibilities Shaun had considered, he never guessed this was the purpose of their meeting. "Well," he answered slowly, wondering where he should even start and how much Aaron wanted to know. "It's kind of a long story."

"I've got plenty of time," Aaron said. "Indulge me."

"I've enjoyed cooking for as long as I can remember," Shaun began. "But it wasn't until the last few months that I realized it was a gift, not just a hobby."

With Aaron's encouragement, Shaun downloaded his journey with Stewart—his tale of awakening to deeper purpose, purging false beliefs, and gaining greater clarity on his passion and gifts. He explained the Six Laws of Conscious Creation. He mentioned that he'd written down his vision of his ideal life, but he didn't share the details, thinking Aaron wouldn't care about that.

Aaron listened intently, and Shaun gained more confidence as the conversation progressed. "And so here I am," Shaun said in closing. "I enjoy working with my clients and helping them find financial solutions. But my heart is taking me in a different direction."

Shaun wondered if he was revealing too much, given Aaron and Brad's friendship. But for some reason he felt he could trust Aaron. "I'm in a bit of an awkward situation now," he continued. "Brad recruited me pretty aggressively, and he's treated me very well. I'd hate to do anything to upset our relationship. But I've tried to make it clear where I'd like to be eventually.

"And honestly, I don't feel quite ready to make the leap anyway. I feel as though I have a lot to learn about business first. I've considered trying to get a job at a restaurant, but I just don't have the resume for it. And even if I did, I'm not sure that's the path I should take. So I keep doing the work Stewart taught me. I take one step at a time. And I'm trusting that the way will open up for me."

Shaun suddenly realized he'd been speaking for thirty minutes; his food sat before him, cold and untouched. "Oh, forgive me," he said, embarrassed. "I've been speaking too much about me. What about you? Are you going to tell me more about yourself?"

Aaron waved away the question. "You've got quite the story, and that's what I came here to learn. Why don't you enjoy your meal? Then I'd like to hear more about your vision."

Shaun typically would have savored every bite, but he was too engrossed in the conversation. He ate quickly as Aaron made small talk. When he finished, Aaron encouraged him to reveal his vision.

"When I was eighteen years old, just after graduating high school, my father scraped up some money and took me on a two-month trip through Europe," Shaun began, laying the foundations. He smiled as he reminisced. "It was a fascinating and unforgettable experience. We moved around a lot when I was growing up, but I'd never been outside the U.S. We started in London and traveled through almost every country in Western Europe and a handful in Eastern Europe. We ended up in Athens and flew back from there.

"I was blown away by the architecture, art, museums, food, everything. The cathedrals and castles were awe-inspiring. The Coliseum in Rome just about knocked me over. We spent hours and hours in museums, and I couldn't get over how much history was crammed into such a small region. I'll never forget the views of the sea from the French Riviera. I remember vowing I'd own a yacht someday and live on the Mediterranean."

Shaun paused, lost in thought, and then leaned forward, excited. "Above everything else," he continued, "what fascinated me most was the vast amount of cultural diversity in Europe. I mean, in the U.S. you can travel from state to state and notice some regional differences, but overall it's pretty much the same. But there . . . you could travel a couple hours and cross a border into an entirely different world.

"I never thought I was prejudiced in the least bit, but I was surprised to discover some minor prejudices as we traveled from country to country. Nothing major, you know, just things you pick up from hearing other people talk over time—about how people from a certain country act, or how people from some other country think. But I felt such a deep kinship with everyone we met."

By this time Shaun was virtually glowing as he recounted his experience, and Aaron studied him intensely.

"There was one experience in particular that I remember like it was yesterday," Shaun said slowly. "I had studied a little bit in high school about the fighting in the Balkans, but I didn't pay much attention to it. It just didn't seem relevant to me, you know? Typical American perspective, I guess. It was on a different planet, and I was living my life.

"But when we were in Greece, we met a Serbian woman selling bread—she spoke enough English to get by in conversation with us. We bought some bread from her and spent a long while chatting with her, and for some reason she opened up to us and shared some of her history. She told us how much she'd suffered through the war. She had lost her husband and two of her three children. All of a sudden that conflict became real to me. It was heartbreaking.

"But then, as luck would have it, the very same day we met a Croatian man and struck up a conversation with him as well. It was just a normal conversation. Three human beings chatting, laughing, sharing. And suddenly I was overwhelmed by this deep understanding that underneath our cultural differences, our language, the color of our skin, we're all the same. We're all human beings trying to get by in this crazy world, doing the best we know, given our knowledge and understanding.

"Here were two people whose history said they should be bitter enemies. But I'd spent time with them both, and I just couldn't wrap my brain around it. I mean, I just knew that if they were to spend time together and listen to each other, they could become friends. I felt this spark inside, something telling me that I would love to somehow create more tolerance and understanding between cultures in the world." Shaun broke from his reverie and laughed. "Naïve and idealistic, I know."

He looked up at Aaron and was shocked to see a tear trickling down the man's cheek.

Aaron wiped the tear away and cleared his throat. "On the contrary, Shaun, it's beautiful. So what does all this have to do with your vision? And where does cooking come in?"

"Well," Shaun explained, "when I got home, that spark was extinguished by all my carefully laid plans. I fell back into the routine of pursuing stability and security, and I kind of forgot about it all. I just wasn't in tune with my intuition. And even if I had been, I didn't have the guts to follow it.

"So anyway, when I went through all these exercises with Stewart, I remembered that experience and that passion was rejuvenated. And that's when the lighting-bolt revelation struck: Why not combine my passion for cooking with my passion for building trust and tolerance between cultures?

"So I developed an idea for a restaurant called Connection Cuisine," he said with excitement. "Imagine walking into a restaurant. You're greeted by a Nigerian man dressed in traditional Nigerian clothing. He escorts you to a table. Before giving you the menu, he gives you some brief background on himself and his country; he tells his story. He hands you a menu, and you find a variety of traditional dishes from all across the world. But the real specialties are fusion cuisine combining different traditions into the same sensational meal.

"There are waiters from other places across the world, also dressed in traditional clothing, who tell their own stories.

"The atmosphere is artistic and eclectic. Art and crafts from various countries are displayed. At one end of the restaurant there's a stage, in front of which is seating for fifty to a hundred people. Live music is performed by individuals and bands on traditional instruments from all across the world. Flamenco, percussion, Celtic, jazz, folk, you name it." He grinned. "You know the Gipsy Kings?"

"Ah, yes," Aaron said. "Ilana and I saw them live at Radio City Music Hall in New York. It was absolutely electric."

"In my dream, the Gipsy Kings perform on opening night."

"I'd pay good money to be there," Aaron said.

Shaun continued, "I know this doesn't create world peace or anything. But I think it's a step in the right direction, however small. Just exposing people to different cultures and perspectives in a warm, safe environment. There's something about food that brings people together. Breaking bread is about more than just feeding the physical body; it's about feeding the soul. I'm not after a Nobel Prize, but I think it could make a difference. And beyond all that, I'd just have a blast creating and fine-tuning the menu. I really believe I could become a world-class fusion-cuisine chef."

"There's no doubt in my mind about that," Aaron agreed, taking a sip of wine.

"So there you have it," Shaun said, shrugging his shoulders diffidently. "I'm sure it's pretty small potatoes compared to what you do, but it means the world to me."

"No, Shaun," Aaron corrected him, "your dream is not small. On the contrary, I'm deeply impressed. I'm touched by your passion, and your vision is inspiring."

"Thank you," Shaun said. He suddenly realized that he'd lost all track of time. He checked his cell phone and was shocked that it read two thirty.

"Aaron, I'm sorry, but I had no idea I'd taken so much of your time. And I really need to get back to work."

"No need to apologize," Aaron assured him. "I got exactly what I came for. I've enjoyed this more than you know."

"Aside from Stewart, I've never shared my vision with anyone else. Well, there is another person who knows part of it, but she hasn't heard the full story. At any rate, it's really refreshing to share it with someone who cares. I've been working alone in developing it for so long. It just feels so good to get it out."

"Thank you for sharing, Shaun," Aaron said. He paid the check, and they walked outside.

"Thank you for lunch—and for listening," Shaun said. "I hope we can meet again sometime."

"Shaun, I promise we'll meet again. I'll give you a call."

Aaron turned and walked to his car, and Shaun stood looking after him, a curious intuition stirring in his soul.

TWENTY-TWO

Two weeks passed, concluding Shaun's second month of cooking lunches for office workers. It was Saturday evening. After a much-needed and refreshing day of mountain biking, Shaun was calculating his earnings for the month. His customer base had grown to twenty-four people over the course of the month, all through word of mouth.

He entered the final numbers into his spreadsheet and whistled softly. He had grossed $3,800, and after $1,861.38 in expenses he was left with $1,938.62 net profit. Not millionaire earnings by any means, but the implications were clear and compelling. If he could earn this much over the course of two months with no advertising . . .

Shaun created a projection spreadsheet and calculated swiftly, changing and analyzing variables, all while being extremely conservative. *Maybe it's time,* he thought, staring at the numbers.

He realized that making the jump to a full-time business would require some infrastructure. For starters, he'd need to formalize his business and get the necessary licenses. He also knew he'd need a commercial kitchen soon; it was becoming increasingly difficult to handle the workload in his apartment kitchen. Still, his confidence was surging. *I can do this,* he kept thinking. Furthermore, something had to give soon. Trying to juggle his full-time job and his side project was beginning to wear on him, and he knew it couldn't last.

On Sunday, after preparing lunches for the next day, he spent the afternoon dreaming and planning. By the end of the day, he had decided to take a leap of faith.

On Monday morning Shaun knocked on Brad's office door.

"Come in," Brad called.

Shaun took a seat and cleared his throat nervously. "So you know how I told you where my passion was leading me?"

Brad's face dropped. "Oh, no. Here it comes. You're leaving us."

"Yes," Shaun acknowledged. "But not immediately. If you're okay with it, I'd like to give you a month's notice to give you time to replace me."

Brad breathed a long sigh and then looked up, smiling. "You know, I never should have let you cook lunches for me or had you cater dinner for the Weisses."

Shaun grinned back. "I guess that's the chance you take with an aspiring chef."

"You've done great work for us," said Brad. "I'm very sorry to see you go. But I suppose it was inevitable. I'm disappointed that we only had you for such a short time, but I understand what you're doing. It was much the same for me when I started this business. I can't blame you."

"Thank you so much for understanding," Shaun said. "I've really enjoyed my time here, and I've learned a lot. I'm sorry it happened this way. I wish I had had more clarity months earlier."

Brad held up his hands. "Shaun, it's really okay. I wish you all the best. I'll support anyone who pursues his passion. And I respect you for giving up what you have here to do it. That takes guts. But I must say I do have one condition."

"What's that?" asked Shaun.

"You have to keep bringing me lunch," Brad said with a grin.

Shaun beamed. "Done."

The next month was frantic, a flurry of activity. In addition to maintaining his regular work schedule, Shaun had agreed to train his replacement, whom Brad hired a week after Shaun gave his notice. After-work hours were consumed with building the basics of his business, as well as continuing cooking for his existing clients. He got his licenses and hired a friend to create a logo, build a basic website, and put together flyers. He also retained a real estate agent to help him find a location for a commercial kitchen. He spent his Saturdays looking at possible locations. Toward the end of the month, he finally found a place in a somewhat concealed strip mall, a restaurant that had shut down just a month previously. He signed the lease papers, torn between feeling excited and worried.

In addition to building his business infrastructure, he also did everything he could to cut his personal expenses. He had already been living on a tight budget, but now he was willing to sacrifice even more. He stopped buying clothes and music and canceled a couple of magazine subscriptions. On the weekend before his final day at work, he downgraded to a cheaper studio apartment just two blocks from his business location.

On his last day of work, Shaun performed his remaining tasks, though he found it nearly impossible to concentrate. At four thirty in the afternoon, Brad invited him to the conference room, where he found all his coworkers, as well as a couple of his clients. Brad had organized a small going-away party. They mingled for a few minutes, with his coworkers and clients filing past Shaun to say good-bye and wish him luck. They gave him a card that they had all signed.

"Can I have your attention?" Brad said. The room quieted. "I just want to say a few words for Shaun." He paused, looking at the floor in thought. Then he looked up and continued, "I still remember the day I quit my last job ten years ago, like it was yesterday. I still remember what it felt like—a combination of irrepressible excitement and awful dread." He smiled, and everyone laughed.

"I knew I was doing the right thing," Brad went on, "but I was scared to death. I had no idea whether or not I could make it. But I believed in myself and I was passionate about my idea, and that belief and passion carried me through. Shaun is showing that same belief and passion, and I admire him for that. I hate to see him go, and I know his clients do too. But as I've already told Shaun, I'll always support anyone's passion.

"So, Shaun, thanks for your hard work. You've done a phenomenal job for us. But I know you have a gift that must be cultivated. I wish you the best of success, and I want you to know that I believe in you."

Everyone applauded after Brad finished. Then he said, "Shaun, any final words?"

"Sure," Shaun said. "First of all, I want to thank you, Brad, for believing in me. You believed in me enough to hire me, and now you believe in me enough to let me go graciously. That means a lot. And thank you all for being so driven and passionate about what you do. I've loved working here. I love the entrepreneurial spirit and how you encourage everyone to think outside the box and innovate. I've had a wonderful experience. And I can totally relate to Brad right now. I'm scared too, but I know this is the right thing to do." He paused and grinned. "And there's a few of you left who aren't buying lunches from me. Now's the time to jump on board before I get too expensive for you."

Everyone laughed and cheered. Shaun said his good-byes. Sure enough, as he was about to leave, two more people asked to be included on his customer list.

He left the office and drove home in a daze. When he got home, he poured a glass of wine and sat on the couch. *From reading a strange Sanskrit word to this,* he thought. *What a ride! But this is just the beginning.*

As the awful realization of what he'd just done permeated his soul, a desperate fear welled up inside him. He caved to it for a few minutes, overwhelmed. But then he forced himself to walk to his bedroom, where he had posted his belief manifestos. He read through them out loud several times before the fear finally started to subside. Feeling his confidence reemerge, he read them again and again, louder each time until he felt strong and whole again.

He was following his bliss. He already had a track record. There was a proven demand for his service. Worst-case scenario, he would learn valuable lessons—and he knew from Stewart's mentoring that knowledge and experience were worth far more than a steady paycheck and benefits. Still, he hardly slept that night.

The next morning Shaun wolfed down an early breakfast. For the first time, he would be preparing lunches for his office customers from his new location. He walked to his new place and felt a burst of pride as he unlocked the door and stepped inside to begin his first official day as a business owner.

He finished preparing the meals by ten thirty. He loaded the containers into his car and rushed to deliver them. After a quick lunch of his own, he hit the streets to hand out flyers and talk to business owners.

To make delivery as easy and time-effective as possible, Shaun worked in a concentric circle around his old office building, stopping at every office complex he could find and speaking to anyone who would let him in the door. At first he was nervous, but he gained confidence by creating a belief manifesto on the spot and repeating it over and over again in his mind. *I provide a valuable service. People want my service. I make their lives better. I am confident and calm when I tell people about my service.*

His approach was to explain to the receptionist what he was doing and ask to speak with the business owner. If he could get in to see the owner or decision maker, he would explain his service, give the person a food sample, and ask if he could pass out flyers to all the employees, or if the business owner would do it for him. A few gatekeeper secretaries wouldn't let him in. Others did, but the business owners said no. Still, he managed to pass out one hundred flyers by five thirty in the afternoon.

Despite his efforts, however, no one had committed to his service. He drove home, deeply discouraged. But his cell phone rang as he drove. He answered quickly, then pulled to the side of the road.

"Hi, this is Shaun."

"Shaun, my name is Jeff. I got one of your flyers today and I'd like to try out your service."

Shaun almost shouted out loud with joy, but he forced himself to remain calm and record Jeff's information. He hung up and then shouted triumphantly, "Yes! One down, a few hundred to go!"

He turned on his computer when he got home and was even more thrilled to discover another request for service in his in-box. Two new customers his first day! He still had a long way to go to be profitable and earn the living he wanted, but it was working.

He quickly responded to his new customer, and then he ate a quick dinner. He was about to go shopping when an idea came to him. He logged back on to his computer, opened his browser, and composed an e-mail.

Amanda,

I can't begin to explain everything that's happened to me since you broke up with me. Suffice it to say that I've learned you were right. I was scared of following my passion and afraid to take risks. And I now know what that fear cost me: opportunity, joy, and fulfillment. And most of all, you.

But I think you'll be happy to know that I'm on a much different track now. I'm now a business owner in Seattle. I moved here to take a new job a few months ago. But then, thanks to some mentoring from a new friend, I got more in tune with my passion for cooking, and I quit my job just yesterday. My business is cooking lunches for office workers and executives. I'm not rich yet, and it remains to be seen if I can even be profitable, but at least I'm following my passion.

I must say it feels good. It's taken me a while to conquer my fears. I've learned that the only true security in life comes from pursuing my passion and living my True Purpose. I really feel like I'm on track with my purpose now. This business is just the beginning of a much larger vision that I'm committed to achieving. Ultimately, I want to own a restaurant that combines my love of cooking with the passion I discovered in Europe.

I want to thank you for doing what you did. I must admit it was exactly what I needed. It compelled me to change my thinking. More than that, it's changed my entire life.

He stopped writing and thought long and hard before continuing. He was afraid of being too vulnerable. But then he decided he had nothing to lose.

However, it does make me sad to think about what might have been. I don't mean to dredge up past pain, and I have no expectations. But I would like to see you again, if you're open to it. Perhaps when I come to visit my parents for Christmas?

Sincerely,
Shaun

TWENTY-THREE

Shaun leaned against the counter and stared out the front window, trying to will customers to walk through the door. A sick feeling hung heavily in his stomach. After five days since opening his café, he'd served a total of sixty-five customers.

What am I doing wrong? he wondered anxiously. *Not enough advertising?* He shuddered to think that was the problem, given that he'd already spent $5,000 advertising his grand opening. *Hasn't my reputation spread by now?*

It had been two months and one week since he'd quit his job to launch his business. The good news was that business was still booming for his lunch delivery service. He was up to 143 customers and growing daily. He'd even hired three employees—a kitchen helper, a waitress, and a delivery driver. He had been so excited about the results that he had decided to expand his business. He had taken over the location of a failed restaurant, so the infrastructure was already built for a small café. It seemed like a natural and easily implementable extension of the business. He simply served in his café the same meals he was delivering to his office workers.

In addition to his advertising costs, he had spent $5,000 updating the interior decor, getting new signage, and buying new equipment. He knew he had a proven product; his lunch delivery customers raved, and his retention rate was enviable. After doing some research, he was confident his prices were more than fair, given his food quality. Still, his café prospects were looking dismal.

He watched Jessica as she washed the table that had just been vacated by their solitary customer. He'd hired her to serve as both waitress and busgirl. Unfortunately, their café revenues weren't justifying the cost, and he feared he'd need to let her go if business didn't pick up.

Two more weeks passed with no increase in traffic. The mornings passed fast and furious as Shaun and his helper, Celeste, prepared the delivery meals. But after they finished by eleven thirty, they sat and waited in their ghost-town café. He was pleased to note that most of his customers returned. But rarely did new customers walk through the door.

Shaun was balancing the books in the office one evening when Mike, his delivery driver, knocked on the front door. Surprised, he let Mike in.

"Hey, Mike, what's up?"

"Shaun, I'm sorry about this, but I'm quitting."

"Quitting? Already? You've only been working for a month and a half. I thought you were happy." The dread Shaun had been feeling from the accounting intensified.

"I *am* happy," Mike said. "It's just that I've decided to go back to school."

"Well, I guess I can't blame you for that. So when will you be leaving?"

"Actually, now. I start school tomorrow."

"What?" Shaun gasped. "You're just going to leave me hanging like that? Why didn't you give me any notice?"

"I just wasn't sure how it was going to work out," Mike explained. "I thought I could keep working with my schedule. But at the last minute

I picked up another class in the morning, and some financial aid came through."

Shaun stared at him blankly in shock and disbelief. It couldn't have come at a worse time. "This is really unbelievable."

"I'm really sorry," Mike said lamely.

"Not as sorry as me," Shaun said with a groan.

When Mike left, Shaun slumped into his chair and dropped his head in his arms on the desk.

The next morning he got up at four thirty, jogged to his café, and began frantically working. By the time Celeste showed up at eight thirty, he was more than half finished with the delivery meals.

"What's this?" Celeste asked as she put on her apron. "You trying to get rid of me?"

"Not at all," Shaun said, pausing to wipe sweat from his brow. "In fact, I need you more than ever. Mike quit on me last night without giving me any notice. So now it's up to you and me to get these prepared *and* delivered. You up for some driving today? You'll get to keep any tips."

"Sure, no problem," said Celeste. "But is this just a temporary thing? I was just hoping to spend more time with you in the kitchen to learn."

"I sure hope it's temporary," Shaun said. "I'll post an ad online today to replace Mike. But for now we'll just have to make do."

They finished preparing the meals, and by ten o'clock Shaun was walking Celeste through the delivery route. She left a few minutes later. Shaun dropped into his office chair and massaged his temples, worried sick that Celeste was going to miss something.

Jessica showed up at eleven o'clock, and they went through their prep routine. They served only ten customers. Celeste returned by one o'clock, looking nervous.

"Shaun, I don't know what happened, but I had six lunches left over. I went straight through the list, just like you said."

Shaun groaned.

"I'm sorry," Celeste said.

"It's not your fault," Shaun said. "We'll figure it out. I'm sure we'll know who you skipped when we get some calls."

Sure enough, all the customers that had been missed called within the next half hour. Shaun apologized profusely to each one, offered them free meals for the hassle, and assured them it wouldn't happen again.

As he hung up the phone from the last call, he thought, *Only two months into this, and my business is falling apart. I need some help.* He wrote an e-mail to Stewart and asked if they could speak over the phone. He spent the next hour preparing the menu for the following week; then he checked his e-mail. He was relieved to find a response from Stewart, saying they could speak that evening.

Shaun spent the afternoon preparing the next day's meals and doing accounting and other paperwork, anxiously awaiting the call with Stewart.

"It's all falling apart, eh?" Stewart asked as he answered the phone that evening.

Shaun was annoyed by his lighthearted tone. "Feels that way," he lamented. "I knew running a business would be hard, but I just feel like I have so many blind spots. I'm losing confidence that I can really pull this off."

"Yeah, I know the feeling," Stewart said. "Have you been keeping up on your belief and alignment work?"

"Yes," replied Shaun.

"Good. No matter what happens, it's critical that you keep that up."

"Well, it's been pulling me through the fear and anxiety so far, but sometimes it feels so overwhelming."

"Running a business really is tough, no doubt about it. Some things get easier as you gain experience and get smarter, and as you learn to delegate and train better. But it will always have its challenges. And that's exactly why the rewards can be so great."

"So what am I doing wrong?" Shaun pleaded. "I'm so confused, because my business took off so fast in the beginning. I thought my café expansion would be a slam dunk, but now it's looking more like a horrible move that's going to drag everything down."

"Shaun, here's the deal: You've learned all the laws, and you're ready to graduate from my mentorship and fly on your own wings. I have plenty of thoughts on what's going on in your business from a practical standpoint, and I know that's what you want to hear right now. But the truth is, what will really pull you through this isn't practical advice, but rather applying the six laws. It's time for you to connect them all and use them together.

"So let's take a step back here and analyze your situation from the perspective of the six laws. You've come such a long way in such a short period of time by living the laws, and I want you to recognize that. And I want you to live them at an even higher level now to get past your immediate challenges.

"Just think: A year ago you were a scared CPA in a job you didn't like, focused on security over everything else. But you chose a different life. You chose the Conscious Creator's life. You chose to live a life of conscious purpose, rather than drifting down the stream of cultural norms. You've chosen passion and mission over fear and security.

"You've discovered and developed your True Purpose. You created a compelling vision, and you've been following it, pushing through obstacles along the way. You know who you are and what you were born to accomplish. You've learned to shed your lower, false self and to think and act from your higher True Self. Are you still living on purpose?"

"Yes, without a doubt," Shaun affirmed.

"And if your café fails, will that knock you off course?"

"It could, I suppose, but I'm not going to let that happen. I know from the Law of Choice and Accountability that I'm accountable for my reality. I can choose my perception of reality and how I respond to it."

"You really have been listening, haven't you?" Stewart said.

"Occasionally," Shaun teased.

"So what would be the most empowering and productive way to view and respond to your current situation?" Stewart asked.

Shaun pondered this. "It would be to see my experience as a powerful way to learn business and success principles. The truth is that no matter what happens with the café, I'm still living my passion, and that's priceless. I'm getting a better and faster education than I could get in any classroom. And even if my café fails, the lessons I'll learn from that will take me that much closer to achieving my ultimate vision."

"Excellent," Stewart praised. "You're absolutely right. Your learning curve is going to be off the charts because you had the guts to take a chance and launch your business.

"With the right mindset, failure is simply accelerated learning. If you learn nothing but that business is hard and you don't want to do it, well, you haven't learned anything useful at all. At the end of each day, the most important question to ask is, 'What did I learn?' The faster you learn the right lessons, the fewer mistakes you'll make and the sooner you'll succeed.

And it all starts with a learning mindset and being teachable. That takes humility and persistence, and you've already proven to me that you have those qualities."

"Thank you," Shaun said. "I must admit it feels good to say, 'I choose to see my current challenges as a positive experience.' Just saying it puts me in a different frame of mind."

"That's what I like to hear," Stewart said. "Maintaining that attitude is precisely what will help you learn the practical lessons you need right now, as quickly as possible.

"And, of course, to maintain that attitude you'll need to continue using the Law of Alignment. You've already been doing that to align your thoughts, speech, and actions with your vision. You've identified and reparadigmed your false beliefs to create new beliefs that serve your True Purpose.

"As you continue in your business, you may feel new false beliefs begin to develop. Most people in your situation learn limiting beliefs, such as 'I'm just not meant for entrepreneurship.' They choose defeat over learning. So how can you use the Law of Alignment to stay on track?"

Shaun thought for a moment. "Well, just like you said, I've already felt false beliefs beginning to form. I can consciously nip those in the bud and choose upward to higher beliefs. I can replace them with belief manifestos and refer to those manifestos every time I feel doubt or worry."

"And how can you know which beliefs are true and which are false?"

"By whether or not they serve my purpose."

"Right," said Stewart. "Actually, a better word than 'true' is 'useful.' You want to cultivate the beliefs that are *useful* for accomplishing your purpose and uproot those that are not.

"But let's make this philosophy even more concrete, because there's actually a dangerous aspect of this law. Many people fall into the trap of believing that positive thinking alone will solve all their problems. This just isn't true. There are forces at play in the universe that trump your positive thinking. You can't simply positive think more customers into your café. There may be external forces that will cause your café to fail regardless of how much belief reprogramming you do.

"So listen carefully: *Truth is what works.* I don't want you to think that living the Law of Alignment means pushing through things that simply don't work in the marketplace.

"So you need to be very discerning about your beliefs. In other words, the naïve student may think that the thought of quitting a project is the product of false, negative beliefs. But in some cases, the false belief is actually misperceptions and flawed judgments about the marketplace. In business, what works is defined by what people are willing to pay for. If you want your business to work, you have to give people what they actually want, not what you think is great or what you *think* they want.

"The process of discovering your purpose is very idealistic. But when it comes to applying that purpose in the marketplace, you have to be very practical. You have to accept that other people have their own purposes and dreams, and that no amount of positive thinking on your part can change market realities. So a significant part of the Law of Alignment is understanding that truth is what works and choosing the right beliefs based not only on positivity and idealism, but also on practicality.

"Lofty dreams and inspiring vision are vital. But understand that there are uncompromising realities to business that must be learned through experience. Your dreams must translate into creating tangible value for others. You must meet a demand and make people's lives better.

"Your dream is what *you* want. But in business you have to translate that into what *other people* want. That sweet spot, where your talents, passions, values, and purpose align with actual market demand, is pure gold. In fact, it's the pot of gold at the end of the rainbow that makes you richer and more fulfilled than you ever thought possible.

"But sometimes finding that sweet spot is tough. That's why Conscious Creators know when to quit, Shaun. And it has nothing to do with giving up on purpose. In fact, it's just the opposite—strategic quitting helps you stay on purpose. To serve your purpose, your beliefs must be aligned with what works in the marketplace. Got it?"

"Absolutely," Shaun said. "Makes perfect sense."

"Now," continued Stewart, "the Law of Alignment will help you adjust your course as needed, and the Law of Faith will keep you motivated and strong to focus on your North Star of purpose and hold the helm through the storms.

"Shaun, I want you to forget about your challenges for a moment and bask in the beauty of what you've created through faith. You have called forth a business from your mind into physical existence. It wasn't there before you envisioned it and acted with faith and courage. And now it has appeared because of the miracle of creation.

"Your life has been completely transformed. You have undeniable proof that you can create the life of your dreams and achieve anything you put your mind to. It's official: *You are a Conscious Creator.* You are living the measure of your creation. You are living a life of design, purpose, and passion, the way *your* Creator intended it to be lived.

"Everything you do from here is the exact same process you've already gone through, just at higher levels. But the more you exercise your faith, the more confident you become to achieve higher and better goals. Faith, like muscles and plants, grows as you exercise and nurture it. Even if you have no prior evidence that you can achieve a certain goal, you can still have absolute faith in the creation process now, because you've experienced it for yourself.

"And no matter what challenges you experience, like the ones you're facing now, you know you have the knowledge and tools to overcome them. You don't ever need to succumb to doubt and frustration again. Things won't always work out just the way you envision them, but you can learn and adjust. You can hold on to your faith through the darkest hours and come out the other side as a conquering hero.

"You can lead others with vision and power. They won't see what you see, but your confidence will be contagious. They will trust and follow you because you will be a rock and a light. You will see a forest where others see nothing but an acorn. But you will be able to paint a vision so clear and compelling and speak with such passion that they will believe in your vision.

"Others will criticize you, but you'll have the strength to ignore them and continue building your vision.

"Shaun, do you remember back when we first met, how I promised you that these laws would give you power?"

"I do."

"And do you feel that power now, despite your challenges?"

"Absolutely," Shaun said. "Honestly, I actually feel kind of silly for even feeling discouraged. Just looking back and taking stock of what I've accomplished is really mind-blowing to me. A year ago I never could have imagined that I'd be where I am today. You're absolutely right—I *know* I can overcome these challenges."

"And what will you do to strengthen your faith?"

"Most important, I'm going to continue revisiting my vision daily. I'm going to imagine my restaurant in vivid detail every morning as I meditate.

I'm going to feel the emotions of the grand opening and hear diners praise my food."

"Good," Stewart praised. "Not only will that help you stay motivated, but it will also help you make better decisions. You act differently and more wisely when you act from faith, living as if your vision were already a reality. The firmer your belief, the more your decisions and actions will lead to the fulfillment of your vision.

"What you think is a failure in your business is actually one decision away from success. If you have faith, it will happen. Shaun, I can promise you that daily visualization to strengthen your faith will do far more for you than if I were to simply give you practical advice about how to run your business."

"I believe you," Shaun said. "I promise to keep it up."

"Excellent. And while you're doing that, remember the Law of Gestation. These lessons you're learning now are your gestation period. This is your time to pay the price and prove that you're worthy of your vision. And you'll pay that price both emotionally and monetarily.

"Speaking of which, it's funny to me how willing people are to spend tens of thousands of dollars on a college education but then are so unwilling to take any chances in life at all. And when they spend money trying to implement business ideas that don't work, they call them failures and can't get over the money that they supposedly 'lost.' It's contradictory.

"You are in the gestation period of your vision. You're in school. Just like formal education, the school of hard knocks requires spending money and time and taking chances. But to those with a learning, persistent attitude, the lessons come fast, and they are far more valuable than anything you'll learn in college.

"And Shaun, don't ever forget to simply enjoy the journey. Don't get so caught up in daily struggles and future destinations that you ignore the wonder, majesty, and joy of the creative process *today*. You are *living* your dream! Savor every single day you spend living on purpose; there's nothing else in the world that can match that feeling. Relish even the challenges, because they make you stronger, wiser, and more creative and innovative.

"See, the fascinating thing about this process is that while you're in the process of creating something, your Creator is in the process of creating something as well: *you*. Ultimately, the Six Laws of Conscious Creation are less about what you create and more about who you become. You have to become equal to your vision, and provided you don't give up in the process, the gestation period molds you into the person you need to be for your vision to manifest.

"And when you become what your Creator desires, which is an individual who will find and fulfill his purpose, often the natural by-product is a wealth of resources and influence with which you can serve more and change more lives. You up for that?"

"Absolutely," Shaun declared. "Whatever it takes. I'm committed."

"That, my friend, is precisely why you are successful. I know you have greater successes in store for you, but right now, today, you are successful because of your mindset. With that mindset, the ultimate results you desire are inevitable. Your dreams *will* become a reality. You will continue gathering power to attract the people, resources, and circumstances to achieve your goals.

"The laws I have taught you are natural laws of the universe. They are the laws your Creator used to create you and the world. The elements have no choice but to obey the Conscious Creator who lives these natural laws. And you have that same power. When you live them fully, the elements have no choice but to cooperate with you to make your dreams a reality.

"Don't ever quit, Shaun. You were born for greatness. You were born to be a Conscious Creator, to manifest your vision and make the world a better place. The world needs your gifts, Shaun. We need you to keep creating."

After they hung up, Shaun lay down on his bed, tired but surging with confidence. He knew what he had to do, and he had no regrets about his experience at all. *What an amazing opportunity to learn and grow and to progress toward my vision,* he thought as he smiled contentedly.

As he lay thinking, a text message came through his cell phone. He retrieved his phone from his pocket and looked at the screen. It was from Amanda.

How's business? it said.

TWENTY-FOUR

Two weeks later, on a Saturday afternoon, Shaun was composing an e-mail to Stewart, informing him of his progress, when his cell phone rang.

"Hello?"

"Shaun, it's Aaron Weiss."

"Hi, Aaron. How are you?"

"Just fine, thank you. So Brad tells me you quit working with him to open your business. How's it going?"

"Much better than I ever expected," Shaun said. "It's been quite the ride. I've made a few mistakes and learned a lot, but overall I'm ecstatic that it's taken off so well."

"I'm so happy for you," Aaron said. "Listen, would you be available to meet with me tomorrow afternoon—say, three o'clock? I've got something for you to consider."

"Absolutely," Shaun said, deeply curious. "Tell me when and where, and I'll be there."

"Do you mind coming to my house? We're on the west side of Mercer Island."

"Not at all." Shaun jotted down the address. "Thank you, sir. I'll see you at three."

Shaun hung up and stared at the phone. *What is this about?* he thought. *What could Aaron Weiss possibly want from me?*

Shaun finished his e-mail to Stewart, then wrote another e-mail to Amanda. They were corresponding somewhat regularly via e-mail now, although Amanda wouldn't commit to a phone call and Shaun tried not to get his hopes up. He slept fitfully that night as possibilities cycled through his mind about why Aaron wanted to meet with him.

He rose late the next day, ate breakfast, and then spent the remainder of the morning preparing his lunches for the next day. After finishing a few loads of laundry, he was out the door by one o'clock, en route to Aaron's house.

As Shaun had expected, Aaron's neighborhood was scenic. Towering redwoods and cedars stood sentry over spacious homes on large, lushly landscaped lots. Shaun pulled into Aaron's driveway and saw that the house, a modern-style home with cedar plank siding and architectural-glass walls, was stunning. Plus, it had a great view of Lake Washington.

"Hi, Shaun," said Ilana, who answered the door. "Come on in."

"Thanks, Ilana," he said as he stepped into the foyer.

"Welcome, and follow me. Aaron's in his office."

Shaun followed her down the hall, admiring the intricate tile work on the floor. Ilana escorted him into a large office. Mahogany bookshelves lined the walls, and the high-end modern furniture made Shaun feel as if he were at a resort. Aaron sat at his desk, his back to the large picture windows that overlooked the lake. When Shaun walked in, he rose from his chair, walked around his desk, and shook Shaun's hand.

"Thanks for coming at such late notice," said Aaron.

"Would you like anything to drink, Shaun?" Ilana asked.

"Water would be fine, thank you."

Ilana left them as Aaron was inviting Shaun to sit down. "Shaun, I've invited you here because I want to tell you a little bit about my story," began Aaron, "because of the vision you shared with me. When I met you at Brad's house, I was curious to know why such an amazing chef wasn't working in a restaurant. I simply wanted to learn your story. And, of course, after your excellent work at the youth home, I figured the least I could do was buy you lunch. But after you shared your vision with me, I realized there was much more to you than just a guy who liked to cook on the side."

"Well," Shaun said modestly, "any depth you've seen in me, I owe to Stewart's mentoring. I don't know where I'd be without him."

Ilana returned with a glass of water and then left them to their conversation.

Aaron continued, "Shaun, my wheels have been spinning ever since we last met. And I've been wanting to meet with you for a while, but I've just had a few loose ends to wrap up. As I told you on the phone, I've got a proposition for you. But first I want to give you some context." He paused. "You've undoubtedly guessed from my accent that I'm not native to America."

Shaun nodded.

"Ilana and I were born and raised in Israel. I came to the United States when I was eighteen. My parents had scrimped and saved for years to send me to college in this country.

"As a young Jewish boy growing up in Israel, I had a best friend named Khalid. He was a Palestinian boy. We did everything together and kept no secrets from each other. We were completely oblivious to the long-standing conflict between our peoples. Our friendship was pure and undefiled by history, and I was naïve enough to think it would last forever.

"Then, shortly after we had each turned twelve, we were both shocked when our parents forbade us from playing with each other. We had no idea what had changed and why we couldn't see each other. So we maintained our friendship secretly.

"But soon, something changed. For reasons I didn't understand at the time, Khalid turned cold. He started making excuses every time I invited him to do things."

Aaron paused for several moments, looking down at the floor, deep in thought.

"I still remember one particular day as if it were yesterday. I had told my parents I was going to the store, but I snuck to Khalid's house and tapped on his bedroom window. He came out and demanded that I leave. I was confused and hurt.

" 'Why?' I asked. 'What is wrong?'

"Khalid was furious. He shouted at me, 'Because you're a Jewish swine and a thief! I never want to see you again!'"

Aaron's face contorted with pain as he recounted the memory.

"I was so confused. It took me several years before I was finally able to understand that Khalid's parents had poisoned his mind with hatred. That was the last time I ever saw my friend."

Shaun listened in rapt attention. "I'm so sorry," he said weakly, not knowing what else to say.

Aaron sighed. "In the grand scheme of things, I suppose it's not even worth noting. Just one tiny interaction between two people who were caught between a vast and unfathomable conflict. But that experience has largely shaped my life.

"You see, when you shared your vision with me and spoke of uniting cultures, you touched a chord deep within my own heart. What you described is exactly what I've been trying to do with each of my businesses since graduating from college. My last business was a language software company. Peace and tolerance begin with communication. My deep desire to bring people together across cultures drove the business. It was more successful than I had even calculated. But it became time to move on, so I sold it. That's why I met with Brad. I'm casting about and doing research to find my next opportunity, and I was hoping he had a few ideas or some potential connections.

"I believe business, more than any other institution, can solve human problems. I believe each human being has a stewardship over everything he or she has been given, including what's inside that person as well as his or her money and material goods. I believe that business should be about more than just seeking profit—that it should be about doing good in the world. I suppose you could call me a social entrepreneur. I've always sought opportunities where I could earn a profit while making society healthier and better."

"You sound like my mentor, Stewart," Shaun said.

"Yes, I've appreciated learning about him. He sounds like a man after my own heart."

"I could arrange a meeting for the two of you, if you'd like." Shaun said. "I'm sure that together you could come up with some phenomenal ideas."

"I'm sure we would," Aaron agreed. "But right now my interest is in you."

"Me?" Shaun asked.

"Yes, you," Aaron assured him. "In the short time we've spent together, it's been obvious to me that you have a powerful mission. You're in tune with your passion and you know your purpose. That's extremely rare."

"Well, I appreciate that, but I still don't see where this is going."

"Shaun, the bottom line is this: I'd like to build your restaurant for you. Actually *with* you, to be more precise."

Shaun gulped slow and hard. "I'm—I'm sorry?" he stammered.

Aaron smiled. "Yes, you heard right. I'd like to build your restaurant. See, it turns out that our passions and visions are very much aligned. I have a weakness for fine food. You have a genius for creating it. And we share the passion for creating greater peace and unity in the world. We're a perfect match. I've thought long and hard about it, and I've made my decision. I've got a bit of money to work with. This won't be my only project, but it's a great one. And I'm certain you're the man to work with."

Shaun was speechless. His head was reeling.

Aaron waited patiently for him to gather his wits.

"Aaron," he began, "I'm flattered that you would think of me. But are you sure you want someone as inexperienced as me? I mean, don't get me wrong, I'm thrilled for the opportunity and I'm confident that I can do this. I just want *you* to be certain."

"I'm absolutely certain," Aaron said. "You work your magic in the kitchen. I'll fund the project and handle the business side of things. I've got a great team already in place to manage whatever project I give them." He smiled again. "So what do you say?"

"What do I say?" Shaun repeated. "*What do I say?* Are you kidding? Where do I sign? This is just a dream come true."

"I know the feeling," Aaron said, smiling. "But let's not forget that this was inevitable. You put your vision in place, and you've been working hard to achieve it. Stewart gave you a guaranteed formula. It's worked for him, it's worked for me every time, and now it's working for you."

"I just didn't expect it to happen this soon," Shaun said.

"Well, understand that we've got quite a ways to go before you're in your kitchen. This will be no small task."

"I understand," Shaun said. "So where do we start?"

"Well, the first thing is for us to agree on terms. Now, as much passion as I have for this project, I'm still a businessman. Since I'm taking all the risk, I think it's fair that I would keep eighty-five percent of the company, and you would get fifteen percent. How does that sound?"

"Aaron, that's certainly generous," Shaun said. "With you funding the whole thing, I wouldn't have expected to have any ownership at all."

"Good, it's decided then," Aaron said. "I'll have my attorney draw up the papers, then we'll start working with an architect."

After brainstorming for two hours, Shaun left Aaron's house in a daze. He sat in his car for several minutes, pinching himself occasionally to convince himself that he wasn't dreaming.

His vision was manifesting.

TWENTY-FIVE

The day of Connection Cuisine's grand opening dawned in rainy Seattle. Unable to sleep, Shaun had arisen long before the sun and had gone for a bike ride. He arrived home by eight, showered and dressed, ate breakfast, and checked his e-mail. A message from Amanda was in his in-box.

Hey Dreamer,

I just wanted to wish you luck with your grand opening. I really wish I could be there. I know you're going to knock it out of the park.

I must say, I'm really proud of everything you've done over the past year. And I'll admit, I'm a little jealous. You're an inspiration. This is SO amazing!

I can't wait to hear how it goes!

Amanda

P.S. I always knew you had it in you.

Shaun smiled and reread the message several times. Amanda had been friendly in their recent correspondence, but never this complimentary and vulnerable. This was a good day indeed.

At nine thirty a.m. he drove to the restaurant. As he made the final turn and the restaurant came into view, he thought his heart would burst with pride. Though they hadn't built a new building, opting to convert an existing one, Aaron had spent liberally. It was everything that Shaun had imagined and more.

The exterior, featuring an open terrace, was the perfect mix of dark wooden plank and magnificent stonework. The interior design was modern, clean, and crisp. Paintings, pottery, tapestries, and handcrafted art pieces imported from across the globe were on display throughout the place. A stage for live music with a dance floor in front of it dominated the east wing of the building.

Shaun was the first one there. He parked his car and stood staring at the building in a reverie. Finally, he walked to the front door and took his key out of his pocket. He felt he would never get tired of using that key to open the door; it was an almost holy experience. He entered and took in the view, wiping away a tear of joy. After several minutes, he walked into the kitchen and started prepping. He was starting much earlier than he needed to; he just couldn't wait.

By ten a.m. Shaun's sous-chef and six other assistants arrived and started helping. Aaron walked through the kitchen doors at ten thirty.

"You ready for this, Shaun?"

"You have no idea," Shaun said.

Aaron laughed and said, "Oh, I think I have a little bit of an idea."

"If I hadn't been envisioning this for the last year," Shaun said, "I'd think I was in a dream."

"Well, now you know for a fact that dreams can come true. Listen,

I've arranged for KING 5 News and a few other TV and radio stations to be here for our opening ceremony at eleven thirty. I hope that won't make you nervous."

"I think I can handle it," Shaun said. It *did* actually make him a little nervous, but his excitement overwhelmed the nervousness.

"Nothing to it. I'll say a few words, then you'll deliver your speech, and we'll cut the ribbon. And then we'll bury you in the kitchen."

"I can't wait," Shaun said.

Aaron left the kitchen, and Shaun continued his preparations, glancing up at the clock every few minutes. At eleven o'clock, Aaron returned.

"Shaun, you have visitors."

Stewart and Melanie walked into the kitchen.

"There you are," Shaun said, taking off his apron and hat. "I'm so glad you could make it."

Shaun and Stewart embraced, and Stewart said, "I'm so proud of you, Shaun."

"This dream never would have been realized without you," Shaun said. "Oh, I'm sorry, have you met Aaron Weiss yet?"

"Yes, we met," Stewart said, smiling at Aaron. "Just like you predicted, it seems we're somewhat kindred spirits."

"I thought so. And has he given you the tour yet?" Shaun asked.

"Not yet," Stewart said.

"Well, follow me. We have just a few minutes before the opening ceremony, but I'd really like you to see this before anyone gets in."

Shaun showed Stewart and Melanie through the restaurant, pointing out his favorite details.

"Shaun," said Aaron, "I hate to interrupt this, but it's time for us to go out there."

Together the friends walked out the front door for the ceremony. Shaun stopped hard in his tracks, astonished to discover a crowd of several hundred people in front, as well as a line of people running down the block and disappearing around the corner. He knew Aaron had hired a PR firm and spent quite a bit on advertising, but this was far beyond his wildest expectations. He almost panicked when he realized they didn't have nearly enough food to serve this many people.

Noticing his concern, Aaron said, "I know what you're thinking, but don't worry about it. All we can do is feed our capacity, and you know you have enough food for that. We'll have to turn away a lot of people today. But that's a good thing. They'll want to try us that much more. Be calm. We'll get through this."

"I'll try," Shaun said nervously.

Aaron had set up a small platform. A red ribbon was draped in front of the door. Several camera crews were set up and poised to begin shooting. Aaron walked to the stage while Stewart and Melanie joined the gathering below. The crowd hushed, and cameras whirred and clicked as Aaron began to speak.

"Ladies and gentlemen, thank you so much for coming out today. A year ago I met a young man with both a gift for cooking the finest food I've ever tasted and a dream so compelling that it was impossible to ignore. I'm thrilled to be a part of making his dream a reality.

"Now, I may be partial. But I've eaten at plenty of fine restaurants in my life, and Connection Cuisine offers the finest. I think you'll agree.

"And beyond the food, Connection Cuisine offers an experience unlike anything else, because of our unique vision. I'll let our cofounder explain that. I don't want to steal his thunder.

"Thanks again for your support. We're proud to be part of the community, and we sincerely hope we can make a positive difference in your lives and in the world. And without further ado, I'd like to introduce you to the young man with a dream, our cofounder and the finest chef I've ever known: Shaun Porter."

Aaron stepped down and the crowd applauded.

Shaun stepped onto the stage and took his notes out of his pocket. He paused for a moment and gazed out into the crowd. As his eyes scanned the crowd, a face jumped out at him. He stared. His heart leaped to his throat. He gulped hard in disbelief. Smiling brightly and waving to him was Amanda.

He stared down at his notes and tried desperately to compose himself. Finally, after what seemed to him to be a very long time, he was able to open his mouth.

"Thank you, Aaron," Shaun said, reading word for word from his notes. "As Aaron said, Connection Cuisine is about more than food. It's about an experience."

Suddenly, he gave a little chuckle, folded his notes, and put them in his pocket. Then he took a deep breath and just began saying whatever came into his head. "When I shared my vision with Aaron a year ago, I was confident I would accomplish it someday. But I had no idea this vision would be realized so soon.

"This really is a dream come true. In truth, the dream is quite simple: I have a passion for fine food, and I have a passion for increasing tolerance and understanding between cultures—for connecting people across the world in more meaningful ways. This restaurant represents a fusion of those passions. We've mixed food, culture, art, music, and fun under one roof to create an unforgettable experience. You'll get the best food, but not only that, you'll learn something about other cultures. We hope you get the chance to break bread with people who are different from you, and we hope you can understand one another better and leave here a more tolerant, more open person. We want to make the world a little smaller and a little better. And a lot tastier."

He smiled, and the crowd laughed.

"I can't begin to tell you how thrilled I am to be standing here today. I look forward to continuing this journey with you. Our doors will open in thirty minutes, and I hope we'll be open for a long, long time."

The crowd applauded again, and Aaron handed Shaun a large pair of scissors. He cut the ribbon, and the crowd cheered.

As he stepped down from the stage, his only thought was to find Amanda, but he was mobbed by dozens of people congratulating him and shaking his hand. He tried to be cordial as his eyes desperately scanned the crowd. Suddenly, he heard Amanda's voice behind him.

"Looking for someone?"

He spun around, and there she was, beautiful, grinning ear to ear.

"I thought you couldn't come!" Shaun said. "I can't believe you're really here!"

"Oh, you know me. I'm full of surprises."

Impulsively, Shaun grabbed her and squeezed. She returned the embrace wholeheartedly.

"Mr. Porter, can we have a minute of your time?" a reporter asked.

"I'm sorry," Shaun said to Amanda. "Excuse me for a moment, will you?"

"Go get 'em, dreamer," she said with a grin.

Shaun spent the next half hour being interviewed by reporters. He was impatient to speak with Amanda, but by the time he was free, it was time to get back in the kitchen.

He found Amanda sitting in a chair on the terrace. "Amanda, I'm sorry," he said, "but I've got to get in there."

"I know. Go do your thing."

"How long are you here? Will I get to see you again?"

"When do you close tonight?" Amanda asked.

"Well, we're supposed to close at ten, but it looks like we'll be later than that."

"Don't worry about a thing. Go have fun. I'll be waiting for you in the parking lot when you're done."

They hugged again, and Shaun rushed inside to start taking orders.

Stewart and Melanie were the first to be served. Shaun wished he could have sat down and enjoyed the meal with them, but with the pressing crowds, the best he could do was break out of the kitchen to bring them their main course.

"Thank you so much for coming. It means the world to me for you to experience this with me."

"We're honored to be here," Melanie said.

Stewart nodded. "You've earned this, Shaun. It's been our privilege to have shared this journey with you."

"I wish I could stay longer, but I'm sure they're desperate to have me back in the kitchen."

"Go," Stewart said.

"Will I see you again while you're here?" Shaun asked.

"Our flight isn't until noon tomorrow. Can we connect in the morning?"

"Absolutely. I'll call you," Shaun said, and he rushed back to the kitchen.

The day passed in a mad and frantic blur. The kitchen was flooded with orders nonstop, which finally started slowing down by ten that night. When they served their final customer at ten twenty, Shaun realized he was drenched in sweat. They locked the doors at eleven forty-five, and Shaun had another hour and a half of cleanup and prep to do. When he finally stumbled out the back door at one fifteen a.m., he was exhausted—but feeling more fulfilled than he had ever felt in his life.

True to her word, Amanda was standing by her car in the parking lot, waiting for him. "Hey," she said, moving to hug him.

"I don't think you want to do that," Shaun replied. "I'm pretty gross."

"I can handle it."

They embraced, and Shaun held her for a long time.

"I'm so proud of you," she said.

They turned and leaned against the car and gazed at the restaurant, deep in thought, enjoying the moment.

"It's funny." Amanda said. "On the one hand, I can't believe how much you've changed. On the other hand, you're simply everything I knew you could be. What happened?"

"It's simple, really. I followed your advice and made a choice to truly live."

MORE RESOURCES TO HELP YOU BECOME A CONSCIOUS CREATOR

Visit www.ConsciousCreatorBook.com to access the following resources:

- ***The Conscious Creator's Reparadigming Journal:*** The journal, available as a digital download for free or a paperback for purchase, is designed to be an indispensable supplement to the book. It consists of complementary content and exercises that will help you discover and articulate your True Purpose, create a vision for your ideal life, identify and replace your false and limiting beliefs, and claim your birthright as a Conscious Creator. *Your experience with this book is not complete without the journal and its exercises.*

- **Thirty-Day Creation Challenge:** The Thirty-Day Creation Challenge is a social challenge designed to prove that you can earn money by following your passion. Anyone who wants to elevate his or her life and enjoy greater fulfillment is invited to join the challenge. Your challenge is simply to earn as much money from your passion as you can within thirty days. On the website you'll find tools and resources to help you maximize the benefits of your experience.

- **Additional Offers and Downloads:** Subscribe to the mailing list and visit the website periodically to get more free offers, tools, resources, and content, and to be informed of events.

RECOMMENDED READING FOR CONSCIOUS CREATORS

- *As a Man Thinketh* by James Allen
- *Man's Search for Meaning* by Viktor Frankl
- *Magnificent Obsession* by Lloyd C. Douglas
- *Think and Grow Rich* by Napoleon Hill
- *Jonathan Livingston Seagull* by Richard Bach
- *Making the Shift* by Wayne Dyer
- *The Law of Success in Sixteen Lessons* by Napoleon Hill
- *Let Your Life Speak* by Parker J. Palmer
- *Loving What Is* by Byron Katie
- *Up from Slavery* by Booker T. Washington
- *And There Was Light* by Jacques Lusseyran
- *A Million Miles in a Thousand Years* by Donald Miller
- *The Greatest Success in the World* by Og Mandino
- *The Greatest Miracle in the World* by Og Mandino
- *Rascal: Making a Difference by Becoming an Original Character* by Chris Brady
- *The Four Agreements* by Miquel Ruiz
- *The Alchemist* by Paulo Coelho
- *The Gift of Change* by Marianne Williamson
- *Uncle Tom's Cabin* by Harriet Beecher Stowe
- *The Giver* by Lois Lowry
- *Fahrenheit 451* by Ray Bradbury
- *Resolved: 13 Resolutions for Life* by Orrin Woodward
- *LIFE: Living Intentionally for Excellence* by Chris Brady and Orrin Woodward

- *Aspire: Discovering Your Purpose Through the Power of Words* by Kevin Hall
- *A Philosopher's Notes: On Optimal Living, Creating an Authentically Awesome Life, and Other Such Goodness* by Brian Johnson
- *The 7 Habits of Highly Effective People* by Stephen R. Covey
- *Psycho-Cybernetics* by Maxwell Maltz
- *The Power of Now* by Eckhart Tolle
- *A New Earth: Awakening to Your Life's Purpose* by Eckhart Tolle
- *Virus of the Mind* by Richard Brodie
- *Business as a Calling* by Michael Novak
- *Destinae* by Roy H. Williams
- *The Richest Man in Babylon* by George S. Clason
- *Thou Shall Prosper* by Daniel Lapin
- *The Soul of Money* by Lynne Twist
- *The E-Myth Revisited* by Michael Gerber
- *Tribes* by Seth Godin
- *Linchpin* by Seth Godin
- *The Dip* by Seth Godin
- *Do the Work* by Steven Pressfield
- *Turning Pro* by Steven Pressfield
- *The Grace of Great Things: Creativity and Innovation* by Robert Grudin
- *The Dialogues of Plato*
- *The Prosperity Paradigm* by Steve D'Annunzio
- *The Element: How Finding Your Passion Changes Everything* by Ken Robinson
- *The Screwtape Letters* by C.S. Lewis
- *FreedomShift: Three Choices to Reclaim America's Destiny* by Oliver DeMille

ACKNOWLEDGMENTS

For helping me discover, live, articulate, and promote the laws of Conscious Creation, my heartfelt appreciation goes to:

My dear wife, Kalenn, who put up with my obsessive quest to discover every positive law I could find.

My parents, Klaus and Eileen, for being my first and forever teachers.

My other parents, Matt and Laurie, who have always believed in me.

Stephen Palmer, who has breathed life into my books.

My business partners and colleagues—Steve Earl, Stephen Miller, Kevin Clayson, Tyler Bennett, Ruben Mena, Ryan Jaten, and Christine Graham.

A special unintended mentor, Lynda, who helped me begin my deeper journey.

My special "life raft" mentors: Garrett White, Heather Madder, Dena Jordan, Brett Harward, and Analee Berrett McDonald.

One of my favorite business mentors, Ed Hoyt.

My first mentor, LeGrand Baker, who first asked, "Who is Kris?"

And most important, my favorite mentor—God.

QUESTIONS AND TOPICS FOR DISCUSSION

1. When Shaun got the e-mail from Amanda breaking off their relationship, why didn't he rush over to her place and propose marriage?

2. After getting Amanda's Dear John e-mail, Shaun wondered: "Aren't I what every woman wants—a reliable guy with a secure job and a promising career?" Is that really what every woman wants?

3. We know that Amanda wanted to get married, and that she felt Shaun was too reluctant to take any risks. Why then didn't she jump at the chance to get married when Jim, who was edgier and more spontaneous than Shaun, proposed to her?

4. What convinced Shaun that Stewart could help him work out his problems?

5. Why did Stewart tell Shaun that he couldn't help people who don't know what they want?

6. Would it have worked out better for Shaun if Stewart had revealed to him in their first session all six of the Laws of Conscious Creation? If so, why? It not, why not?

7. Stewart said one major difference between unconscious creators and Conscious Creators is "their understanding of beliefs and truths." He said unconscious creators assume their beliefs are truth, but that Conscious Creators see the limitations of beliefs and strive to upgrade their beliefs to truths. Do you feel your approach to your beliefs is that of an unconscious creator or a Conscious Creator?

8. What are some things that can help someone tell the difference between beliefs and truths?

9. During those years when he worked as a certified public accountant, what kept Shaun from realizing that his real passion was for cooking?

10. Stewart talks about cognitive dissonance—discomfort from having two conflicting beliefs. Can you think of any subject about which you have a feeling of cognitive dissonance?

11. Stewart talks of a sweet spot, the intersection your dreams and what the public, the marketplace, wants. Steve Jobs found a sweet spot. He wanted to make and sell a user-friendly computer that non-techies would use at home. And people wanted it. Henry Ford's dream was to make good low-priced cars. He produced the Model T. People wanted it. Sweet spot. Can you think of other examples?

12. What do you think Aaron meant when he said that money he made in various ventures didn't really belong to him and his wife?

13. Stewart emphasizes the importance of "living your True Purpose" and "following your passion." How many present-day well-known people can you think of who seem to be living their purpose and following their passion? How many throughout history? Conversely, can you think of any people who did not live their purpose or follow their passion, either because they didn't realize what it was or because they made a decision to follow other pathways?

14. What do you believe is your passion and True Purpose?